Beautiful
California Deserts

"Learn about America in a beautiful way."

# Beautiful
California Deserts

Concept and Design: Robert D. Shangle
Text: Paul M. Lewis

Second Printing May, 1981
Published by Beautiful America Publishing Company
P.O. Box 608, Beaverton, Oregon 97075
Robert D. Shangle, Publisher

Library of Congress Cataloging in Publication Data
Beautiful California Deserts
1. Deserts—California—Pictorial Works. I. Lewis, Paul M., 1922—
2. Natural History—California—Pictorial Works.
GB615.C2L48   500.915'4'09794   79-14890
ISBN 0-89802-067-0
ISBN 0-89802-066-2 (paperback)

Copyright © 1979 by Beautiful America Publishing Company
Printed in the United States of America

Photo Credits

ROY BISHOP—*page 23; page 29; page 35; page 42; page 43; page 48; page 50; page 58; page 60; page 61; page 63; page 64.*

JAMES BLANK—*pages 20-21; page 28; page 34; page 44.*

BOB CLEMENZ—*page 46.*

ED COOPER—*page 54.*

JOHN HILL—*page 17; page 18; page 30; page 33; page 38; page 47.*

ROBERT SHANGLE—*page 26.*

JERRY SIEVE—*page 19; page 22; page 27; page 31; page 32; pages 40-41; page 45; page 49; page 51; pages 52-53; page 55; page 59; page 62.*

Contents

The Fragile Desert... 7

The Mojave Desert... 9

The Colorado Desert... 13

Joshua Tree National Monument........................... 65

Death Valley National Monument......................... 67

The Fragile Desert

In the past few dozen years, California has experienced a change of attitude regarding its deserts. At one time the arid reaches in the south and southeast of the state were considered something to pass through as quickly as possible. But in recent times the vast and empty deserts have become destinations in themselves as people in increasing numbers learn what the old-timers were saying all along: there's something special about the desert.

To the early explorers and pioneers, the deserts of California were indeed fearsome barriers. Many a traveler through the terribly hot and arid Colorado and Mojave deserts spent the trip wishing he had never made it. Oxcarts and stagecoaches had a rough time negotiating the trackless alkali basins or climbing through the rocky mountain canyons. It was a dangerous trip, and the bleached bones of man and beast bore witness to many a tragedy.

Nowadays, the uncertainties of travel are all but eliminated. Driving across the desert on a smooth highway is really no challenge at all providing one has taken reasonable precautions about the working order of his vehicle and established how far it is to the next filling station. The roads have brought towns; and the roads, towns and automobiles have done much to allay the fear that the desert has traditionally inspired in people. Travelers found that once they had a choice about whether or not to go to the desert, and how long to stay there, they could relax and enjoy what it had to offer.

At the same time that advances in roadbuilding, transportation and air conditioning were making it easier to enjoy the desert, growth in population on the coast was supplying plenty of people to do the enjoying. One of the very curious aspects of man in general, is that as soon as he builds himself a city, he starts looking for a way to get out of it. Man hungers for civilization, but he thirsts for wilderness; and the desert is wilderness supreme. It's a place people can go where, for a while, they will not be just tiny voices lost in the general din. The desert is a place where man is a visitor—a vulnerable one.

Nowadays, the danger is less *from* the desert than *to* it. Now that the curse of traveling through, or even living in the desert has been lifted, there is little to prevent its overpopulation. Water is a problem, but perhaps not an insurmountable one; and we've already built desert cities that defy the summer sun to do its worst. The Colorado Desert is already experiencing urbanization on its western mountain fringes. Towns in the canyon oases are growing rapidly. Soon communities will be spreading farther and farther into parts of the desert once considered too harsh for human activity of any kind.

Populating the desert may not be harmful. But too heavy a concentration of people and towns could wreak havoc not only on the desert environment but on the wilderness-seekers who are trying to get away from concentrations of people. In California some determined steps have been taken to assure that the desert will remain a place of refuge. Although they are heavily used in some seasons, the preserves and park areas of the desert are now the real oases offering modern man asylum from the burdens of life in the frantic twentieth century. More parks, both national and state, are in the planning and the ''maybe'' stage.

But there is danger to the desert: for all its apparent harshness, it is a fragile place. Without healing rains and lush vegetation to cover scars in the land, the desert is slow to repair itself. Showing off this fragile beauty in a book is a calculated risk; and we can only hope that the person who is inspired by these photographs to visit the desert will also be inspired to be a careful visitor. In this way he will have the satisfaction of knowing that the rare and very special magic of the desert will still be there to work its spell after he has left.

The Mojave Desert

California's biggest desert is fairly easy to locate and define. The Mojave is in southeastern California, east of the southern Sierra Nevada, and east and north of coastal Southern California. In the south, where it begins to sink down toward sea level, it is no longer the Mojave Desert, but the Colorado, a low-lying basin that occupies a relatively small triangle along the border with Mexico. A man-made boundary defines the area of the Mojave Desert fairly accurately. Huge San Bernadino County is the political entity of California that *is* the Mojave, give or take a few tag ends of the western and southeastern desert.

The Mojave is distinct from the Great Basin deserts to the north and east, not only in its landforms but in some of its life forms. It is nearly all high country—between 2,000 and 5,000 feet. It slopes toward the Colorado River, which forms the biggest stretch of its eastern boundary. It is cut off from Pacific moisture by continuous mountain chains on its western and southern borders; its annual quota of rain is about two inches. The innumerable basins of the desert are broken up by frequent low mountain ranges, mountains that were once much higher, worn down through the eons while ice-age lakes were occupying the desert valleys. The Mojave, in places, has an aspect that is scary to anyone who is not ordinarily a desert-watcher: although the desert sage and the creosote bush are widespread and hardy residents of the dry Mojave, even they are absent from some areas, and the glittery salt flats seem barren and inhospitable.

This is what must occupy the thoughts of travelers coming into the state from the southeast and leaving it by the same route. Even in these times of fast cars and super-highways, drivers prefer not to make the crossing from Los Angeles to Las Vegas or Kingman in the heat of a summer day. The route from the Nevada line to Barstow, now Interstate 15, is the same as that of the pioneering Mormons when they crossed on their way to the founding of San Bernardino. The bleak Mojave landscape and the desert heat has remained the same from that day to this. Dehydration and heat exposure are just as dangerous on a super-highway as on a trackless waste being negotiated by oxcart.

The Mojave seems old, lifeless in its more typically arid parts, but it is really neither the one nor the other. In geological time it is comparatively recent, having been covered by ancient seas more than once until it later was raised up into highlands with steep mountains and deep canyons. It had lakes, or remnants of them, as recently as five hundred years ago. And in the Mojave, as in other desert country, the generally sterile view conceals a great gathering of plant and animal life. There's even a resident population of human beings. The eastern desert between I-15 and I-40 from Barstow to the border is a vast area of many different landscapes, and several tiny communities harbor a total of about 250 individuals in an area of two million acres.

Barstow, a mining town around 1880-1890, and now a railroad center, is headquarters for exploratory trips into this huge eastern desert wilderness. The roads into the back country between the two big highways are infrequent, but well maintained. Surrounding Barstow are several landmarks of interest. Twelve miles to the northeast is Calico, a ghost town that was once a mining camp, now restored to its former image. The Calico area is being actively explored by archaeologists. To the northwest about thirty-five miles, in the Opal Mountain vicinity, a visitor may still see Indian petroglyphs at Inscription Canyon.

East of Barstow some twenty miles one may visit Afton Canyon, possibly the most beautiful gorge in this part of the desert. The canyon is one of the very few places where the shy Mojave River comes out of hiding below the surface of the desert and actually behaves as normal rivers do. The on again-off again river rises in the San Benardino Mountains to the west and flows now and then to its destination, Soda Lake, a vast sink south of Baker. The Mojave, for all its eccentric behavior, has been enough of a river over the years to serve as a travel route through the desert for Indians, Spanish and American explorers, and mountain men, not to mention more recent participants in the desert experience. But the presence of the river is of course the main reason for the beautiful canyon.

Running roughly parallel to I-40 (Barstow to Needles), old US 66, now called the National Trails Route, offers a highly scenic alternative south of the freeway from near Barstow to Essex. About twenty miles out is Newberry, at the Newberry Mountain oasis, a rare event in this parched territory. The area's principal inhabitants are desert bighorn sheep and wild burros. Around Essex, herds of cattle are pastured on the sparse vegetation of greasewood and bunchgrass. South of sunblistered Amboy, Bristol Dry Lake's powdery salt flats produce nothing but mirages. A mile or so south of Amboy is a volcanic cone 200 feet high rising out of surrounding lava beds. Another phenomenon of volcanism is Mt. Pisgah, a deeply cratered symmetrical cinder cone in the midst of an extensive lava field thirty-some miles east of Barstow.

From Baker, a little town midway along I-15, a road takes off in a southeasterly ramble past the enormous dry sink of Soda Lake, where the Mojave River empties its almost nonexistent waters. Baker has authentic connections with borax mining in Death Valley to the north. It is at the crossing of the late Tonopah and Tidewater Line—the T & T was the borax carrier from Death Valley to the Union Pacific main line in the south. The very first borax haulers were, as everybody knows who ever listened to the marvelous old Death Valley radio series, the "twenty-mule teams." The teams each pulled 20 tons of borax ore through the valley's Wingate Pass to the railhead at Mojave, 160 miles away.

Some general features of this area south of Baker are extensive and impressive sand dunes, lava beds, and desert mountains. Twenty-five miles farther east on I-15, another paved road leads south past the lofty fault-block Ivanpah Range to Cima. The east-central Mojave has many of these fault-block mountains, the older ones showing the wear and tear by being up to their fractured shoulders in their own alluvial waste. The Ivanpah is an exception to this, like the high and steep Providence Mountains a short distance to the south.

The precipitous Providence range is the backdrop for the loneliest state preserve in California. Deep in this eastern reach of the Mojave, it is far from any other park in the state system. Perhaps that is appropriate, because the Providence Mountains State Recreation Area is the home of Mitchell Caverns, light years away from most other park themes. It's closer to the clouds—when there are any—than to anything else; its elevation is 4,300 feet, overlooking a long panorama of desert valleys and mountains to the south and east. The caverns themselves are giant chambers formed out of carboniferous limestone. They contain the extravagant stalactite and stalagmite formations associated with such limestone caverns. There are numerous entrances, as well as the ashes from the fires of presumed ancient cave dwellers. The limestones of the cave area are also rich carriers of fossil evidence of the sea life that flourished in ancient times when the high desert was lower and wetter.

Nearby, reachable on a county road by following the frequent signs, is a Bureau of Land Management campground at Hole-in-the-Wall, a region of striking geologic formations created by the erosional forces of water and wind on volcanic rock. This high desert—mostly above 3,000 feet—is a very strange place, its barrenness a dramatic brew of lava flows and cinder cones, its sand dunes creating fantastic patterns of light and shadow as the day flows over them. The mountains are beat-up, fractured, and crumbly. Some of them, like Cima Dome, have given up their angles and edges for a weird-looking granitic symmetry. The bulge of Cima Dome is so smooth it can be ridden to the summit. In the Cima Dome environs is a Joshua tree forest. Tall cholla cacti spread their spiny round arms in the sunlight; the barrel cactus hides in the rocky corridors; and springtime brings lush yellow carpets of wildflowers.

One of the largest of the Mojave cactus families is the chain, or "jumping" cholla. It grows to 12 feet high with a thick main trunk and great "chains" of spiny arms clustering on the branches. One doesn't mess with these chollas—they get their moniker as jumpers because of their propensity for breaking off, when touched, at a joint in the "chain." The joint is then attached, by means of the formidable spines, to any luckless critter that brushes against it, be he man or beast. Once imbedded, a cholla spine is difficult to remove. But this is all quite in keeping with the tenacity of desert life—success in the desert is measured in adaptation and resourcefulness, and this is just the cholla's way of propagating itself.

Most of this wild and varied desert between the two interstates, with Barstow at the apex, is under study by the Bureau of Land Management for a two-million-acre national preserve. It would seem a wise move, before the fragile desert structures become damaged by overuse or misuse. California's deserts are parceled out into Death Valley National Monument, Joshua Tree National Monument, and Anza-Borrego State Park, plus the huge enclaves of the various military branches in the central desert.

In the far western Mojave is a very different part of the desert. Antelope Valley is one of the more cultivated 1,500 square miles in the whole Mojave, agriculturally speaking. Such a development would be likely for several reasons, one of which is rainfall. The valley is situated where the Tehachapi and San Gabriel mountains come together in a rain-producing configuration; the amount is not a whole lot more than the rest of the desert gets, but enough to be significant. Then, too, the mountains, receiving the additional rainfall that mountains do, produce runoff that adds up to greater stream flow and a higher water table. But one of the most telling reasons for the growth of farming in the valley is what's just over those San Gabriels that border the valley on the south: the mega-city of Los Angeles.

The growth of Los Angeles has pushed some of the farming that used to be carried on near the coast into the trans-montane valleys like Antelope. This is not to say that agriculture is something somebody just thought of a few years ago in

Antelope Valley. The growth of Southern California at the end of the last century helped to start grain farming, primarily wheat. The first farm boom turned into a "bust" a few years after it started because the weather turned extremely dry and irrigation water was inadequate. But since the 1920s dry-farming techniques and improved pumping machinery have established the valley as an important supplier of farm produce and grains. Antelope Valley, however, still has occasion to display its true desert nature. About half of the 75-mile-long valley is under cultivation (and even bidding for industrial plants), but near Lancaster, the valley's big town of 30,000 population, Joshua trees testify by their strange posturings that this is still the Mojave Desert. And the desert is still in charge during the valley's celebrated spring displays of wildflowers, like those seen on the sere eastern reaches of the Mojave when conditions are right.

The Mojave Desert is not, of course, all in California, but enough of it is to call it a California desert. But not all of the desert in California is considered to be in the Mojave's realm, to wit: the Colorado Desert and the Death Valley area. Each of these deserts has its own chapter in this commentary. But up along the Sierra's east face is an 85-mile-long trough that is, like Antelope Valley, wetter than the lands to the east. And its water, like that of the southern valley, is a direct result of the proximity of the mountains. Although the Sierra blocks off a lot of the rain, in compensation it supplies abundant water by virtue of the mountain streams that feed the Owens River, which runs the length of the valley. Before the City of Los Angeles early in this century built its 223-mile-long aqueduct to siphon off the Owens River (drying up Owens Lake in the process), the valley had a rosy future as farmland.

The main activity here is now sheep and cattle ranching—the same as it was before irrigation agriculture was begun in the valley. However, another industry has sprung up that is related to Los Angeles in another way. The big city's growth has fostered the importance of Owens Valley as a way station for vacationers from the coast headed into the eastern canyons of the High Sierra. The valley is also a thoroughfare for traffic from the south coast to points east, such as Death Valley, and north such as Reno. The communities of the valley are reaping the benefits of this growing trade. Bishop, the principal Owens Valley town, is now a busy tourist center, headquarters not only for desert visitors, but for those interested in penetrating the White Mountains and the Inyo National Forest. Lone Pine, down the valley from Bishop serves as a launching pad where mountain odysseys into the Sierra are organized and equipped. Lone Pine is the eastern entry to the Sierra's loftiest peak, Mt. Whitney (14,494 ft.). It is also a gateway to Death Valley, directly east over intervening valleys and mountains via scenic State 190.

The Colorado Desert

If a desert can be presumed to have luck, then the Colorado Desert of southeastern California can be called lucky. It is one of the hottest and driest deserts of all, but had the good sense to grow up next door to that big and mighty river, the Colorado. Fault-block mountains on the west side—the so-called Peninsular Ranges—furnish ground water, too. By making use of the available water, man has turned a large part of this dry waste into one of the most agriculture-intensive parts of the earth's surface. But other parts are still as deserty as any sandy wastes that ever bedeviled Beau Geste and his fictional colleagues of the French Foreign Legion.

The two now-famous irrigated valleys or basins, Imperial and Coachella, can and do outstrip about any other farming area you can think of. They have the double advantage of fertile alluvial soil and a year-round growing season. Imperial Valley is the bigger area, with some 500,000 acres under cultivation from the southern shores of the Salton Sea to the Mexican border. It produces a wide range of crops, from livestock feeds to fruits and nuts. The 80,000 or so people who live in the valley make their living in some relationship to agriculture. Coachella, the narrow trough that reaches into the northwestern part of the Colorado Desert, is higher and more scenic, with an apron of bleak and beautiful mountain ranges. Coachella Valley's attention is fixed on accommodations as much as agriculture, proof of that being the existence of Palm Springs, that instant oasis that was more-or-less created (in the 1930s) out of the need for Hollywood's affluent to camp out in style in the desert. Palm Springs is no longer quite the exclusive hideaway it once was, having become too popular for that. Since the birth of Palm Springs a string of other resorts have grown up to service the nomads from the coastal plains who travel State 111 between Palm Springs and Indio.

The Colorado is a young desert, younger than the higher Mojave to the north, for instance. Its high mountain perimeter and undulating floor suggests this. The tall, sharp-edged mountains that enfold it on the west, and the lower ridges of the north and east will one day, give or take a few million years, be whittled down to low, rounded hills of sand-dune size. Then it may fit the description usually accorded so many of the older desert areas of the world—unrelieved monotony. Maybe by that time the sea will have moved in again and converted the whole basin to an annex of the Gulf of California.

Even so, the low-lying basin has in this century come close to joining that Gulf on the south. Around 1905 the Colorado River flooded into the sink and created an instant sea when farmers attempting to divert waters of the big river for irrigation wrought better than they intended and things got a bit out of hand. The resulting puddle has since shrunk from its girth at the time of that cataclysmic birth. But it is still about forty miles long and up to eight miles wide. The basin that the Salton Sea occupies was once filled, and more, by an ancient body of water whose surface was a thousand feet higher and reached into the San Jacinto Mountains. When the sea evaporated it left behind in the San Jacintos extensive beds of oyster shells and shark's teeth. Shell fragments are found all over the Coachella Valley today. The odd name of the valley is believed to have come from a misrendering of the Spanish *conchilla* (little sea shell).

The Salton is getting to be one of the world's saltiest seas, having no outlet and being the beneficiary of salts washed from the soils of irrigated areas all across the desert. The irrigation water that adds the salts also insures that the saline Salton remains a sizeable sea. It seems to have stabilized at its present shoreline and now has become a prime recreational lake serving the nearby multitudes of coastal Southern California. The Salton makes a fine wintertime—or even summertime—playground for the refugees from that crowded paradise. In the manner of more conventional resorts, the shores of the Salton are sprouting businesses catering to those who come to sail their boats on the briny shallow and fish for whatever swims in that unlikely desert sea.

The Colorado Desert is many things. If a desert is to be called a "waste," then it must be recognized that such a waste is not a monotone thing of little interest of value. The most interesting variations on the "empty desert" theme probably occur in Anza-Borrego State Park. Anza-Borrego's various terrains occupy a half-million acres in the western part of the Colorado Desert. The state park is probably the finest desert preserve in existence anywhere. But the point is that here, as in any unaltered desert, man is normally just a short-term visitor. The brutal demands that such an environment makes are discouraging to extended residence by a thirsty species like human beings.

Anza Borrego is bigger than all other California state parks put together. Its size is probably made necessary by the increasing use that Southern Californians are making of desert areas in the cooler seasons. The park includes lands near sea level and up into the 6,000-foot range. The latter desertscape would be among the probing mountain fingers and canyons of the western periphery. The park is criss-crossed by roads, most of them the tracks-in-the-desert kind that are suited best for four-wheel-drive vehicles. The real exploring is done, of course, where there are no roads at all, via two legs, backpack, and canteen. The canteen is vital, although at certain times in certain seasons there is a chance of finding water in mountain and canyon recesses or at other scattered oases.

Park Headquarters, a man-made oasis, is near Borrego Springs, another man-made oasis, on an enclave of private land within the park. One may rough it in comfort in the headquarters area, which has all the usual camping amenities; or may rough it in luxury in Borrego Springs, guest-ranch style. But to really rough it, there is the whole huge Anza-Borrego preserve to choose from—camping being permitted anywhere.

Exploratory trips are in almost infinite supply in Anza-Borrego. The short and easy ones are to the palm oases of the San Jacinto Mountain canyons, where places like Palm Canyon and Borrego Canyon display large stands of Washingtonia and California palms. Some of the more remote areas, as in the rugged Santa Rosa Range, require traveling to the end of a road and hiking in. One such trip is to Rockhouse Valley, a lonely place of dry washes, big boulders, and narrow canyons where the ruins of gold miners' rockhouses can still be seen. The park is so big, there are many places like this that most visitors never get to. In the more southerly reaches, accessible from State Highway 78, are valleys and canyons and hidden washes distributed among the Vallecito and Coyote mountains. Anza-Borrego is authentic desert that puts the visitor and camper on his guard. Even though there are some concessions to convenience and safety, such as paved roads here and there, and park rangers who patrol for people in difficulties, resourcefulness is the most important commodity a visitor must bring with him if he is to explore the beautiful and brutal desert wilderness of Anza-Borrego.

The eastern part of the Colorado Desert in California (some of it is in Mexico) is fiercely hot and arid. Variously called the Bard Valley and the Yuma Valley, it is separated from the rest of the Colorado and from the deserts to the north by rings of mountains and hills. One of the notable barriers is the famous Sand Hills, built up of sand blown east by winds. They rise as much as 200 feet and reach north 40 miles to the Chocolate Mountains. What would be an empty wasteland is saved from that disagreeable prospect by the nearby Colorado. The river not only waters the fertile Imperial and Coachella valleys of the central desert through a canal system, but makes agriculture feasible in this southeastern corner. A big block of land here is devoted to the Fort Yuma Indian Reservation, farmed by the Indians since the 1880s. The reservation as originally established in 1884 took in 48,000 acres, covering nearly all of the valley, but the northeasterly half was soon opened to non-Indian homesteaders. Crops and farming conditions are similar to those of the Imperial Valley.

One of California's potentially priceless desert parks has recently (in the 1960s) been created in this Colorado River borderland. Picacho State Recreation Area is situated on terrain that divides the Colorado and Mojave deserts. Consequently, it has a truly remarkable range of environments. Its interior is the true desert, where water is nonexistent. But its river frontage—about eight miles—is thick with vegetation, with lakes and sloughs created when the Colorado was backed up in 1938 behind the Imperial Dam some miles farther south. The river lands harbor a heavy population of wildlife, including coyotes and waterfowl. Travel through primitive Picacho requires either a very rugged vehicle (for dirt roads), two rugged legs (for no roads), or boats, rugged or not, for the lakes.

Spiny cholla cactus

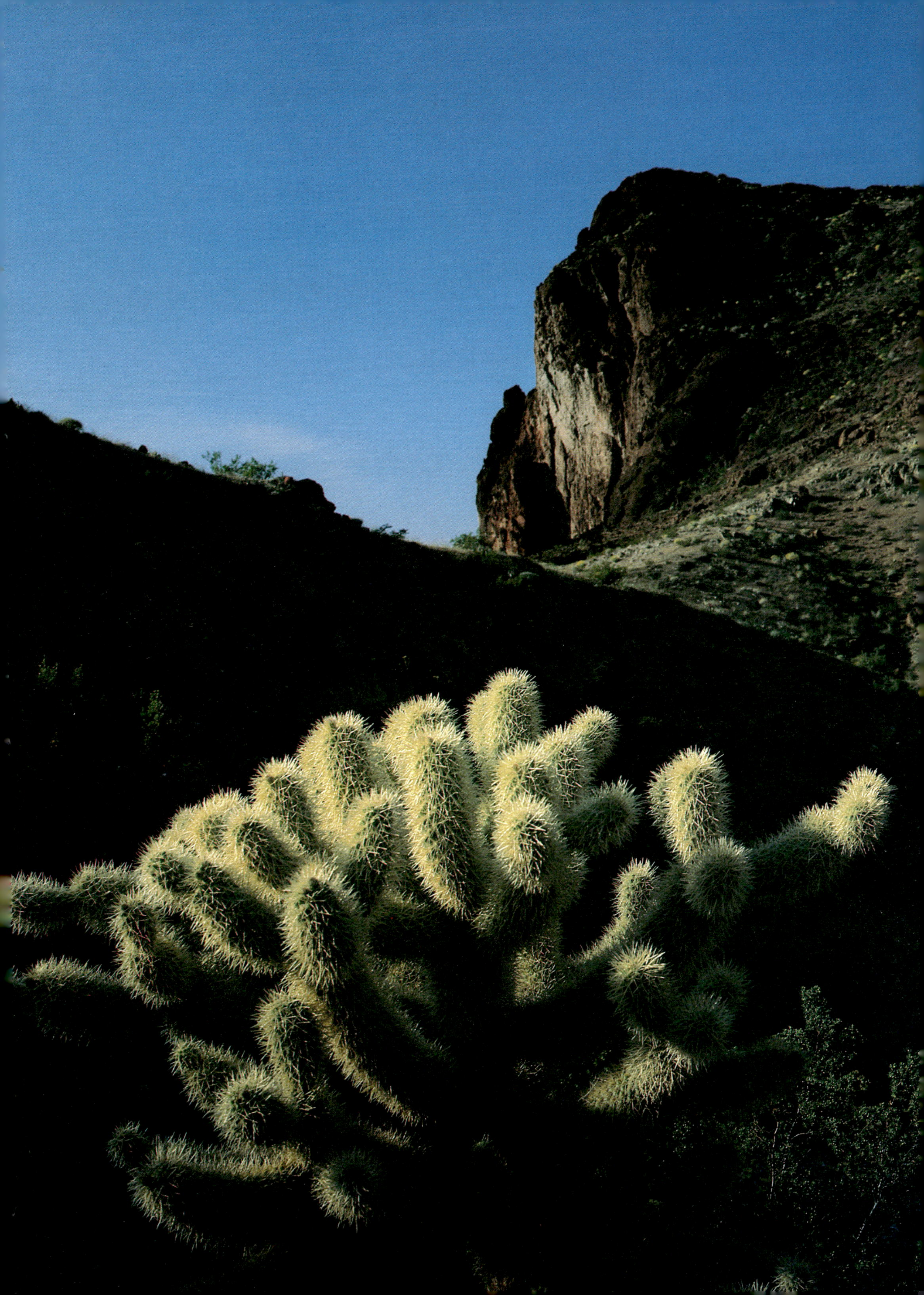

Whipple Mountains northwest of Parker Dam

Dante's View, 5,475 feet above the salt flats of Death Valley
(Following pages) Anza-Borrego Desert

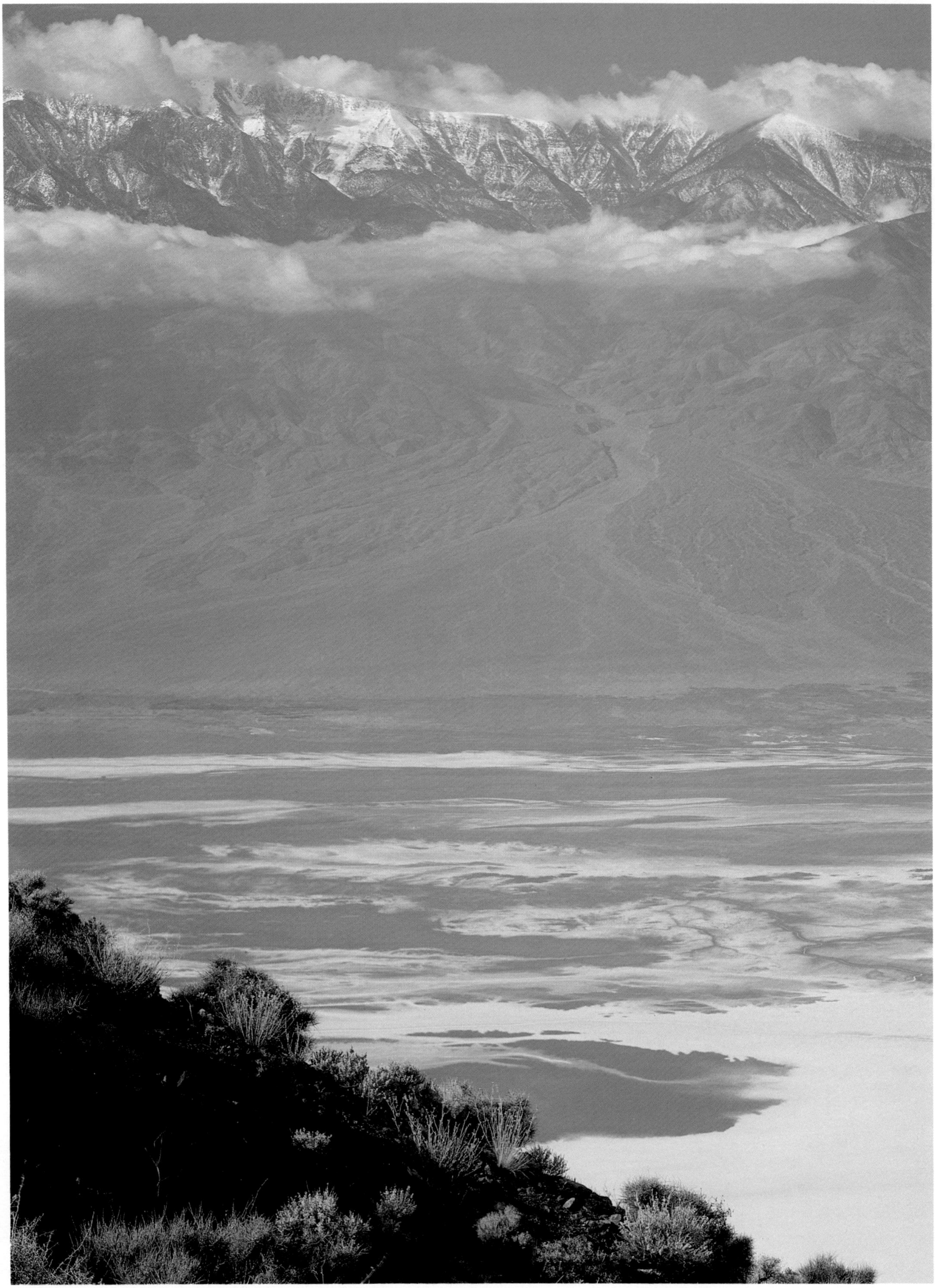

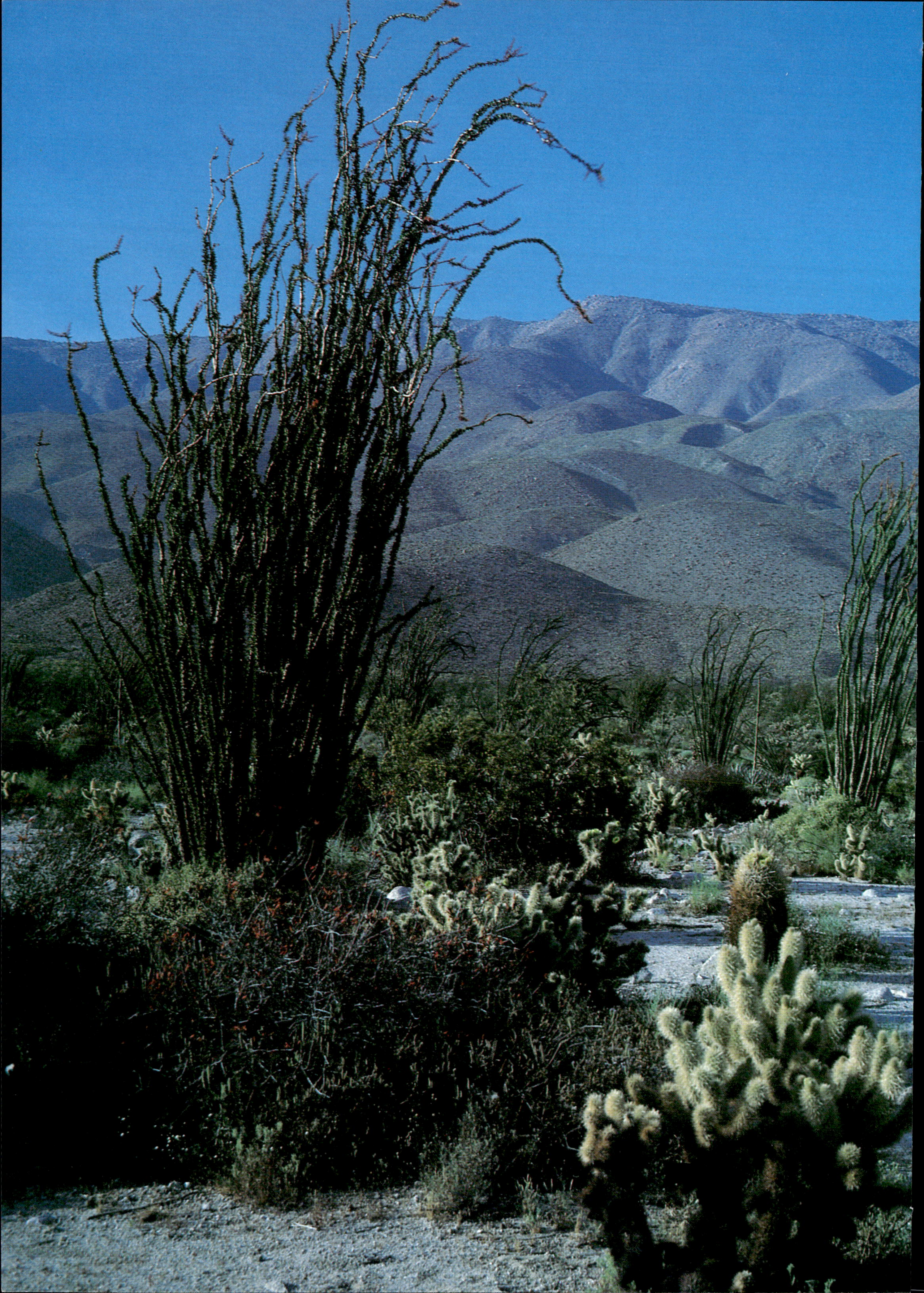

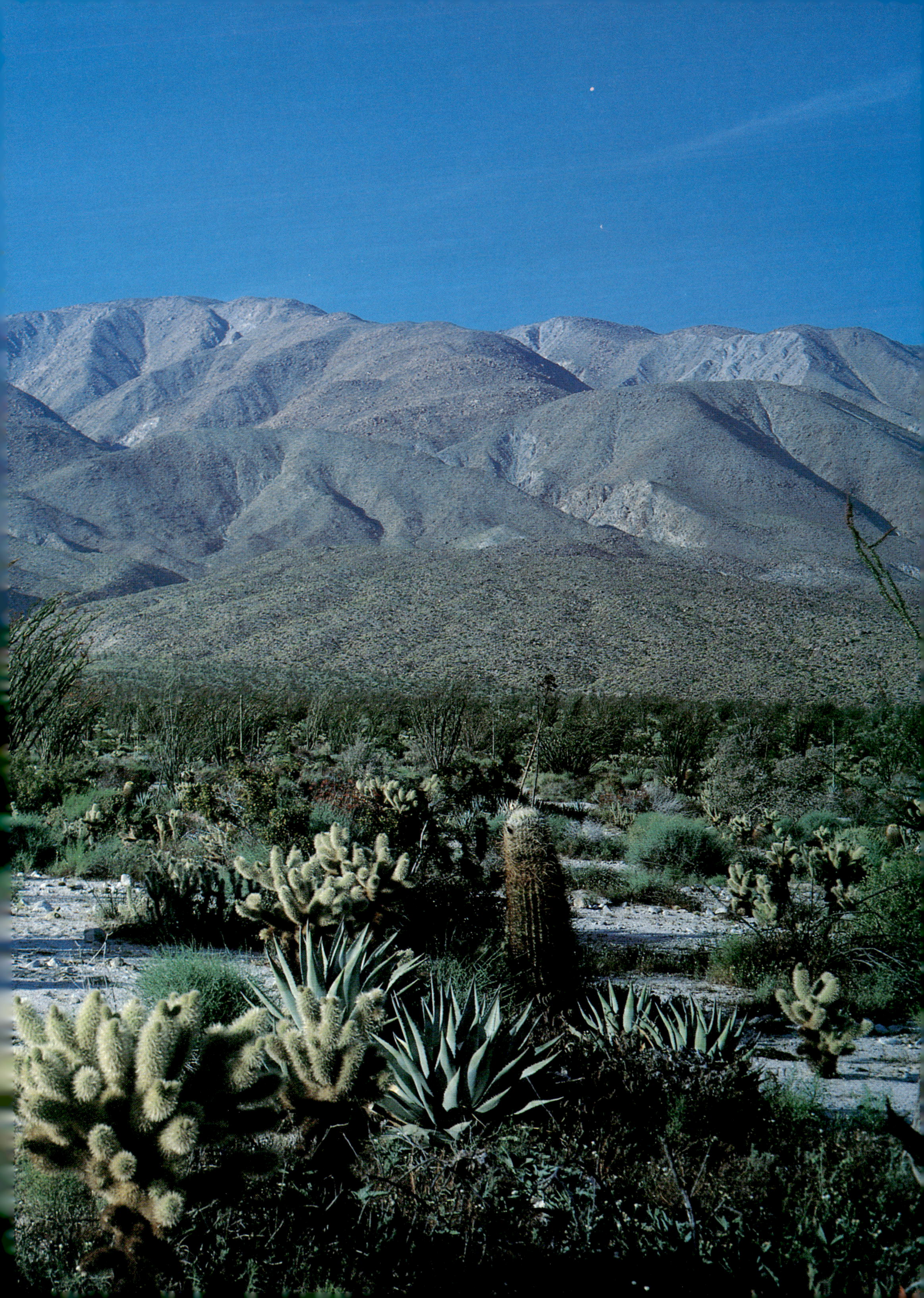

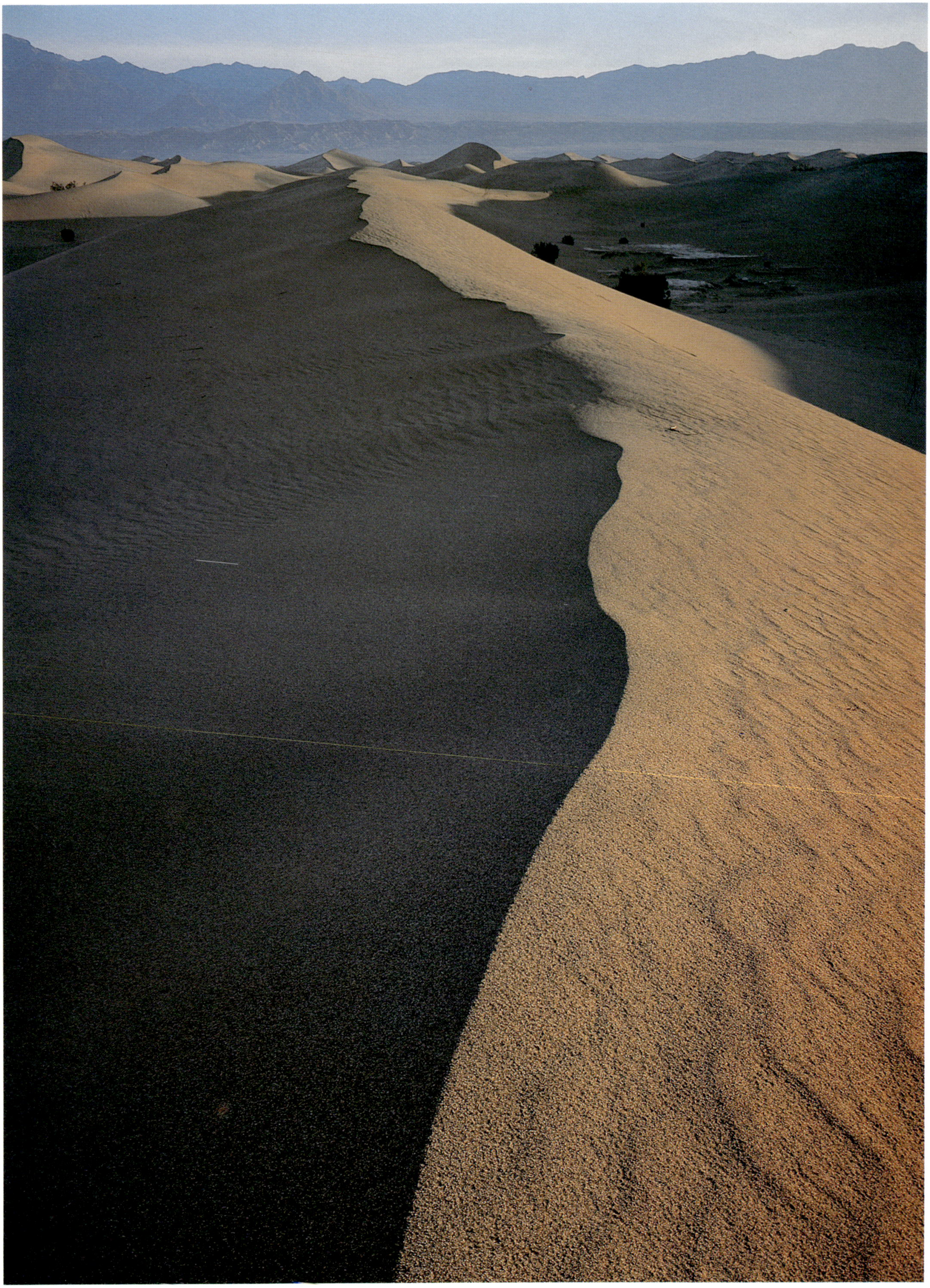

Yucca blooms, Joshua Tree National Monument
(Following pages) Badlands, Death Valley National Monument

Mesquite Flat Dunes, Death Valley National Monument

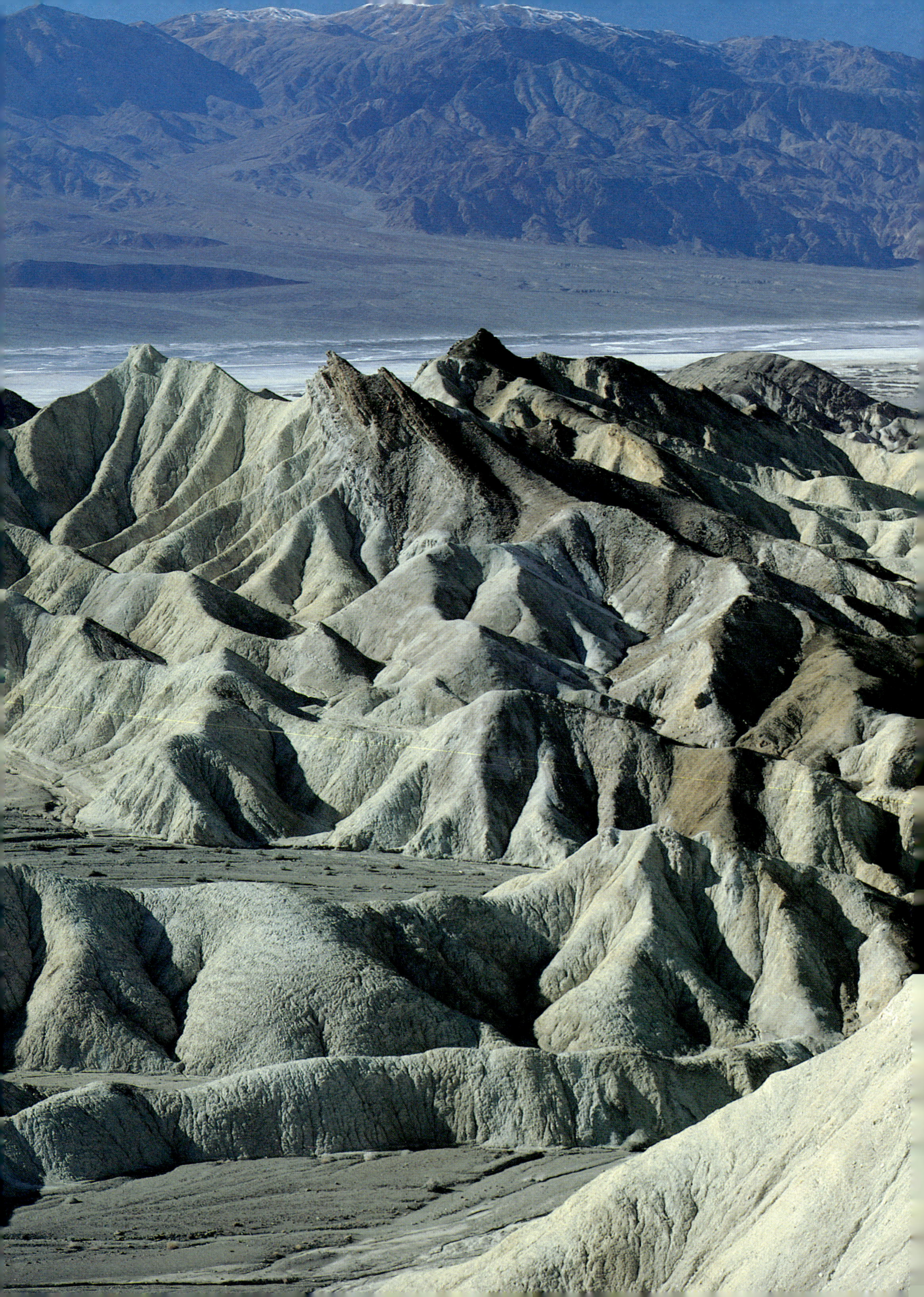

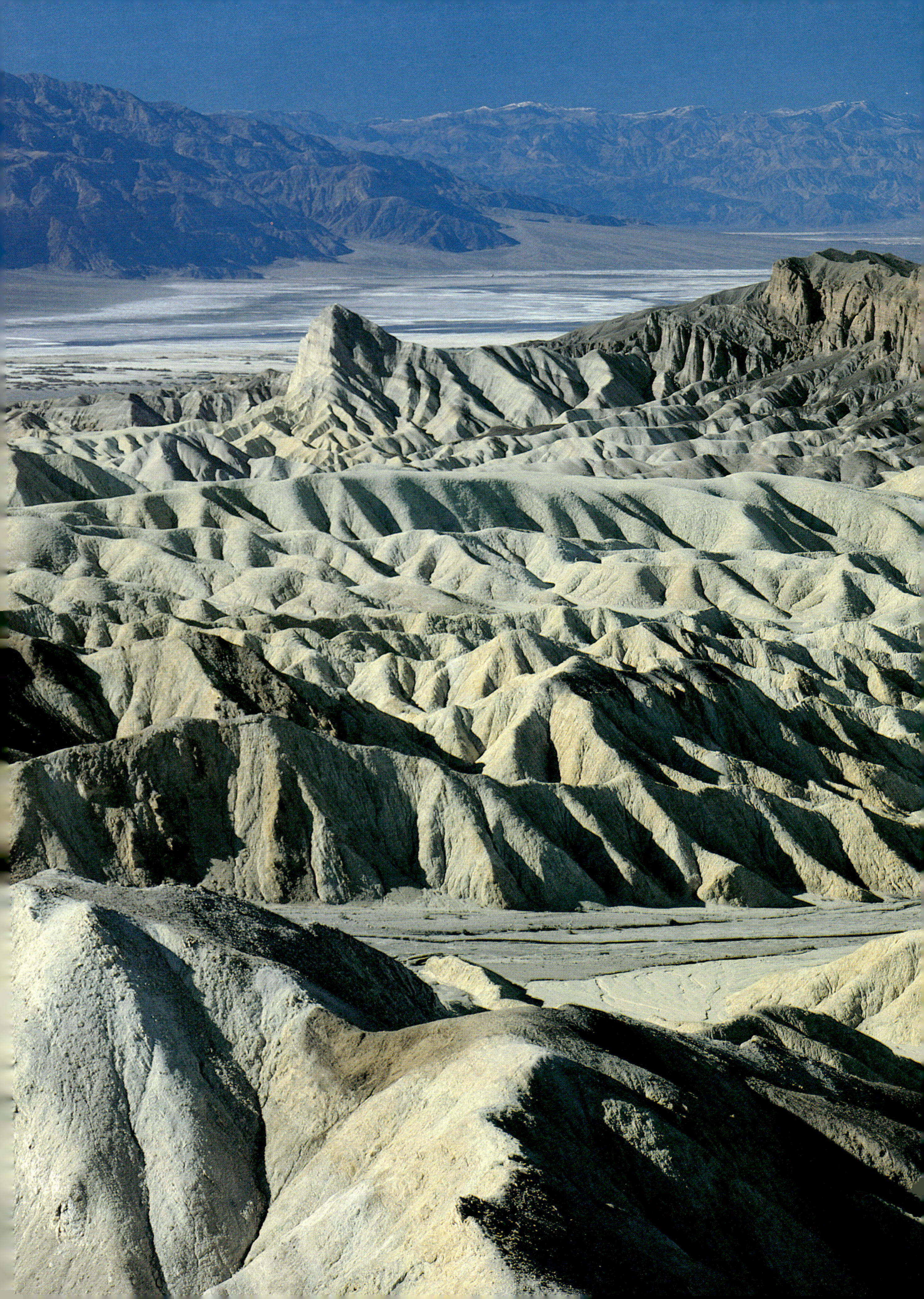

Hedgehog cactus

Zabriskie Point, Death Valley National Monument

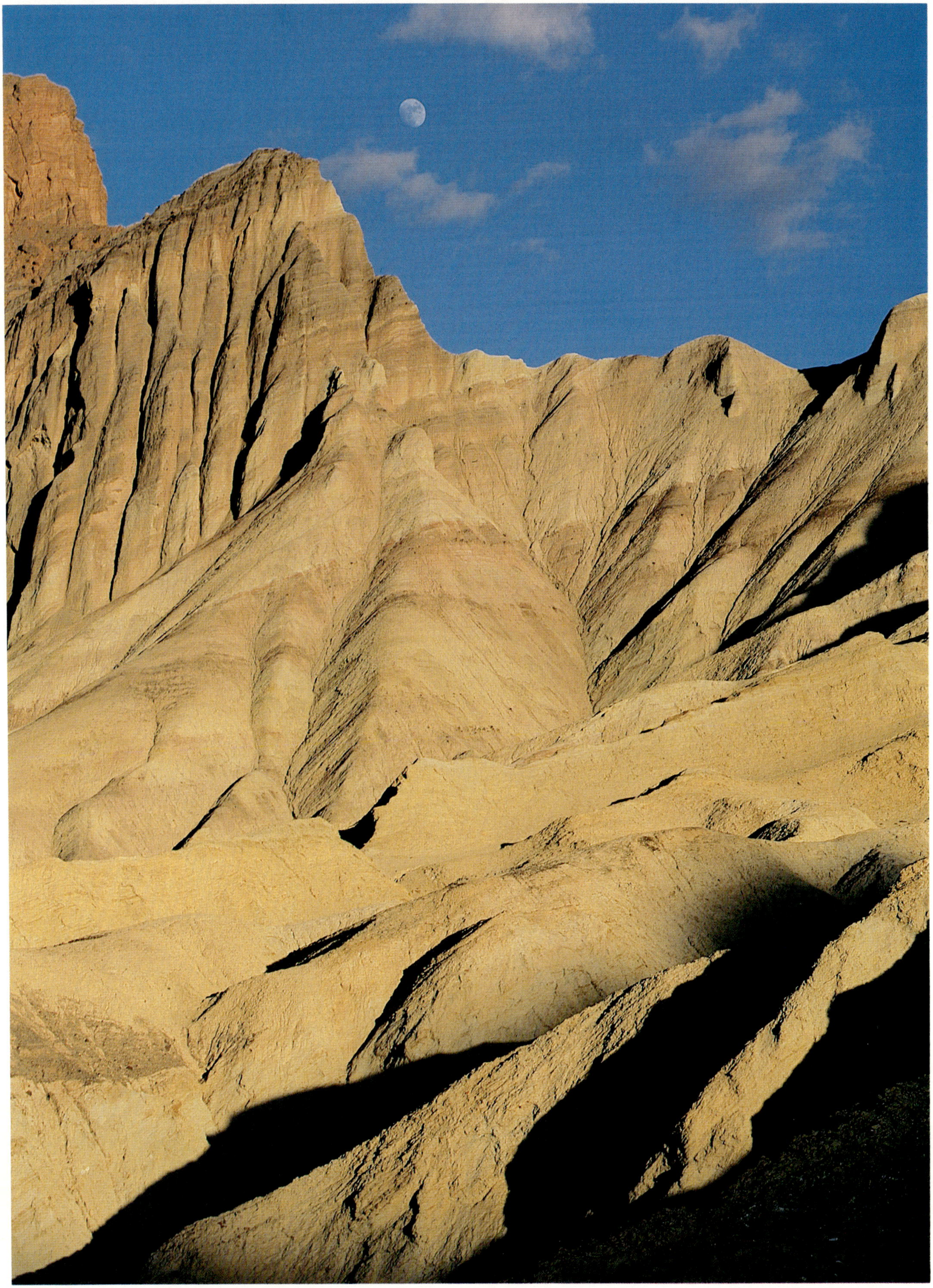

A southern California desert

The yucca in full bloom, Joshua Tree National Monument

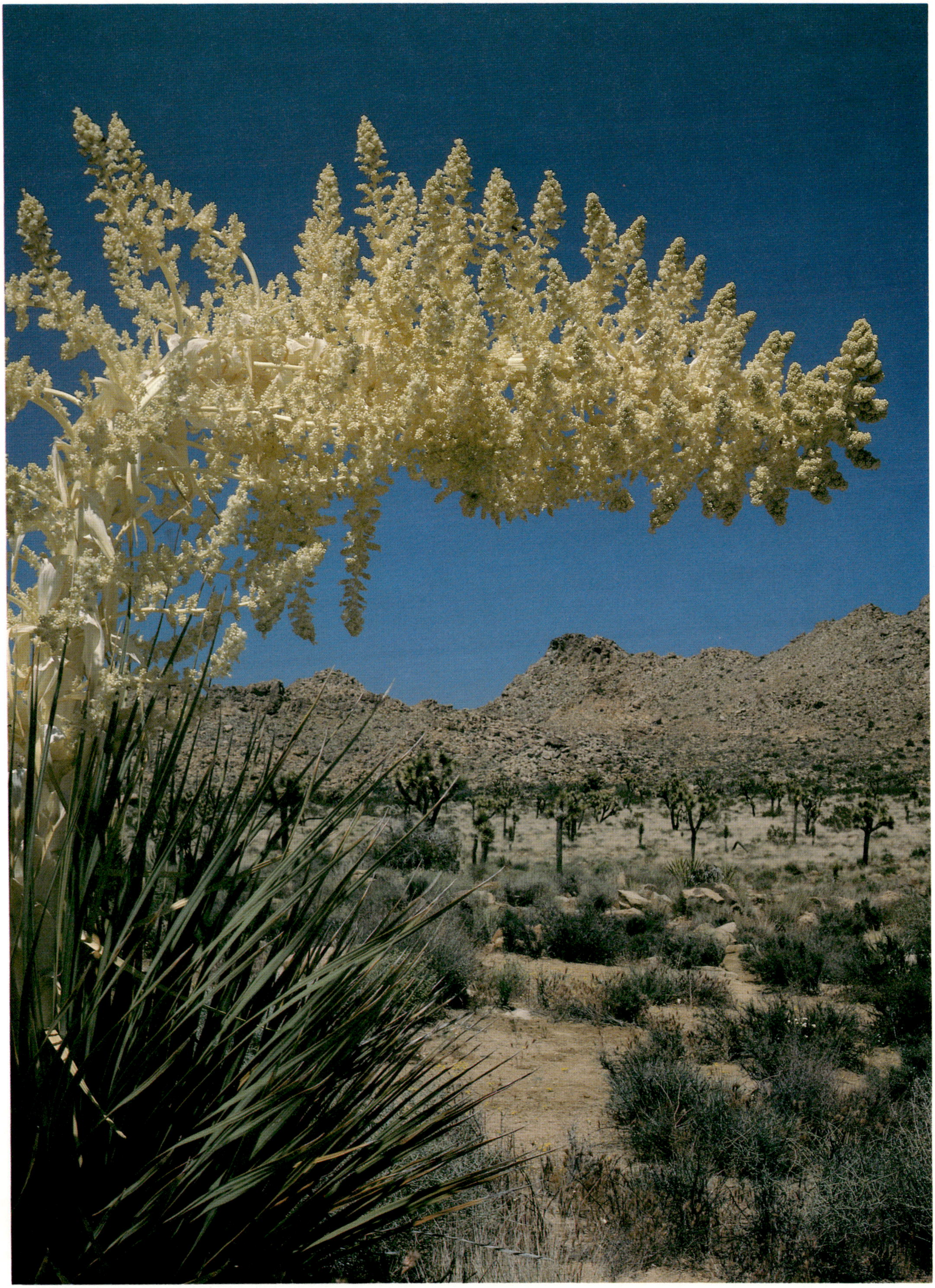

Whipple Mountains

Joshua Tree

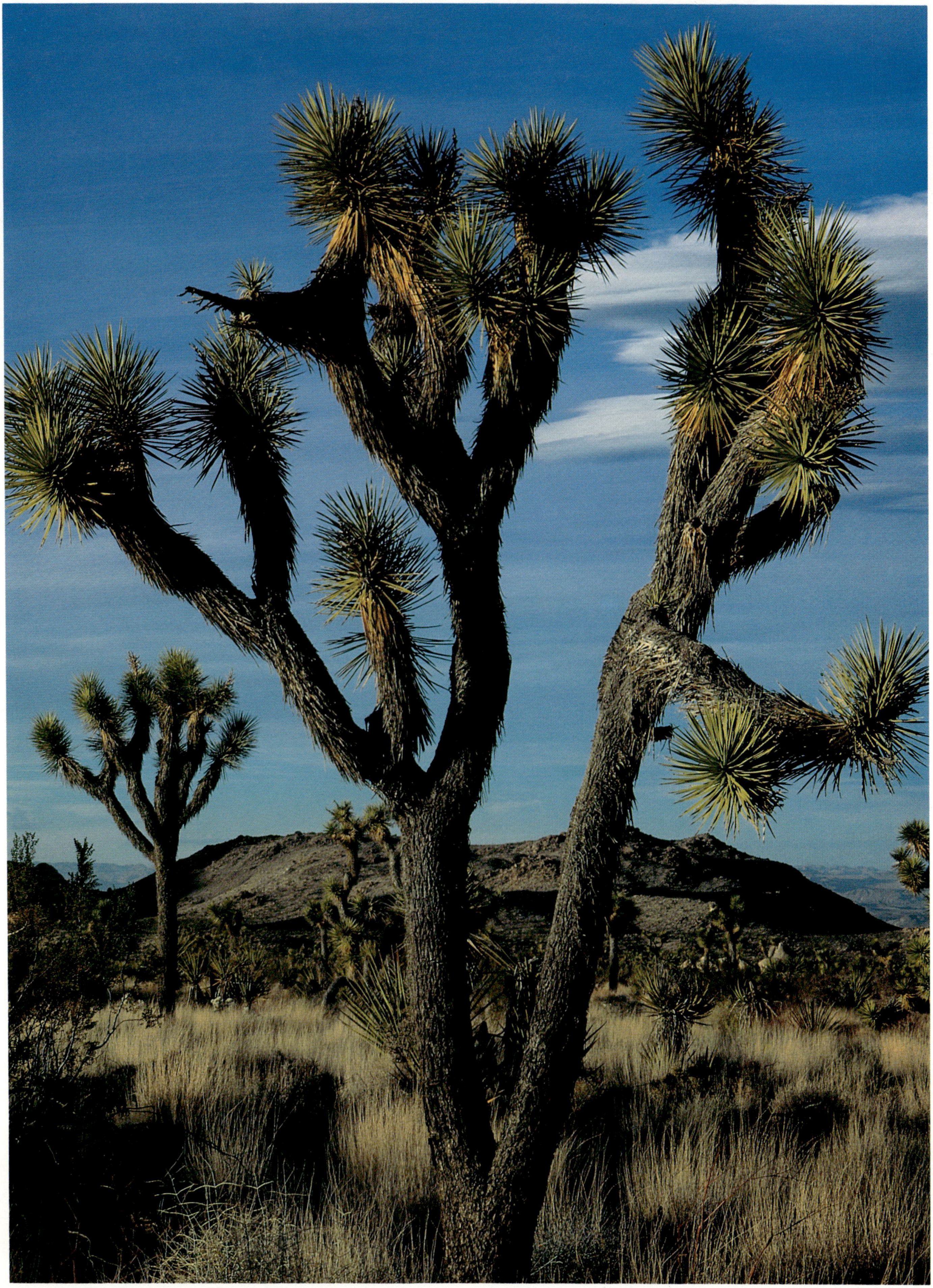

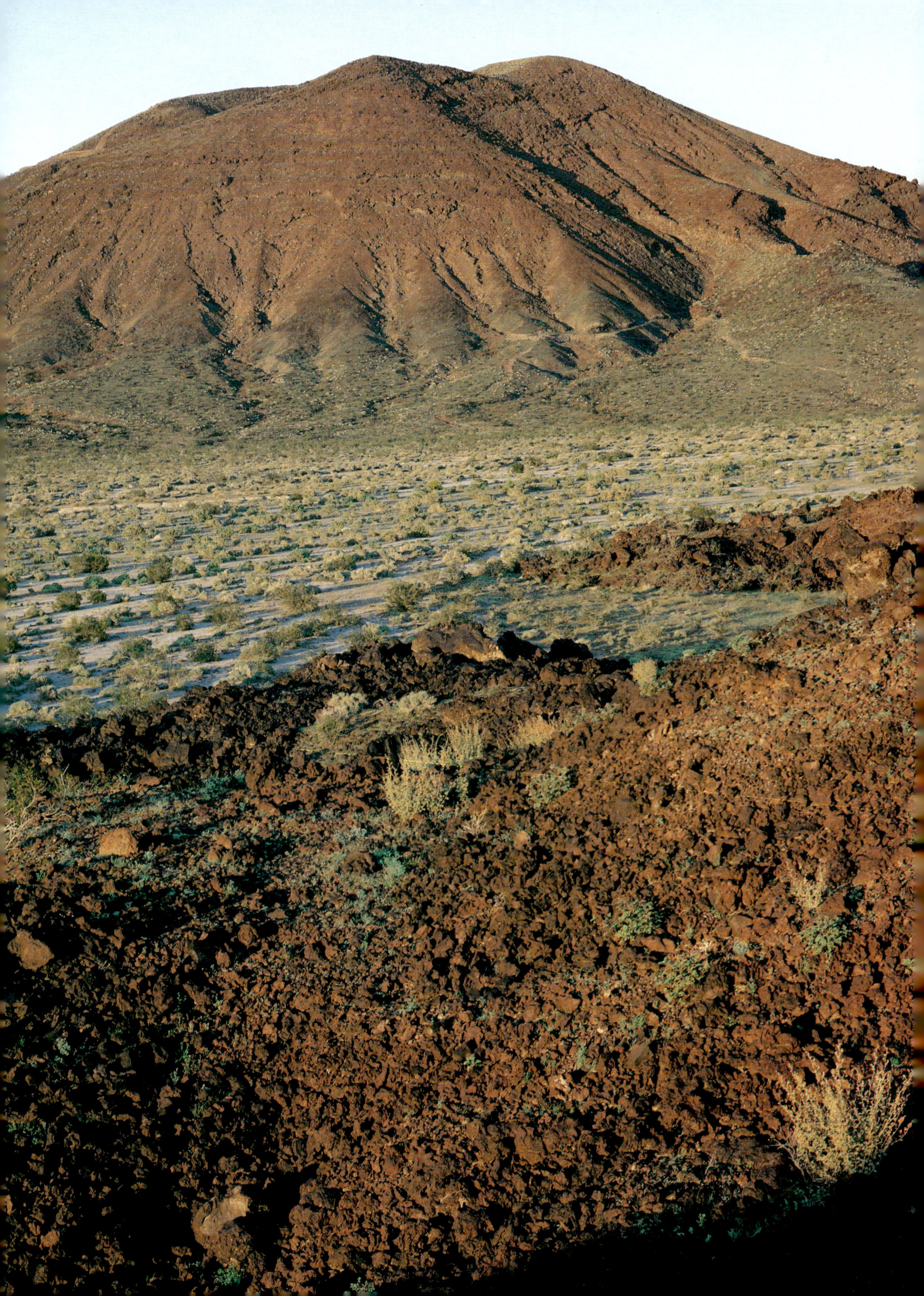

Colorado River north of Blythe

Devil's Playground, Mojave Desert

Spring in the Anza-Borrego Desert

Moonrise, Joshua Tree National Monument

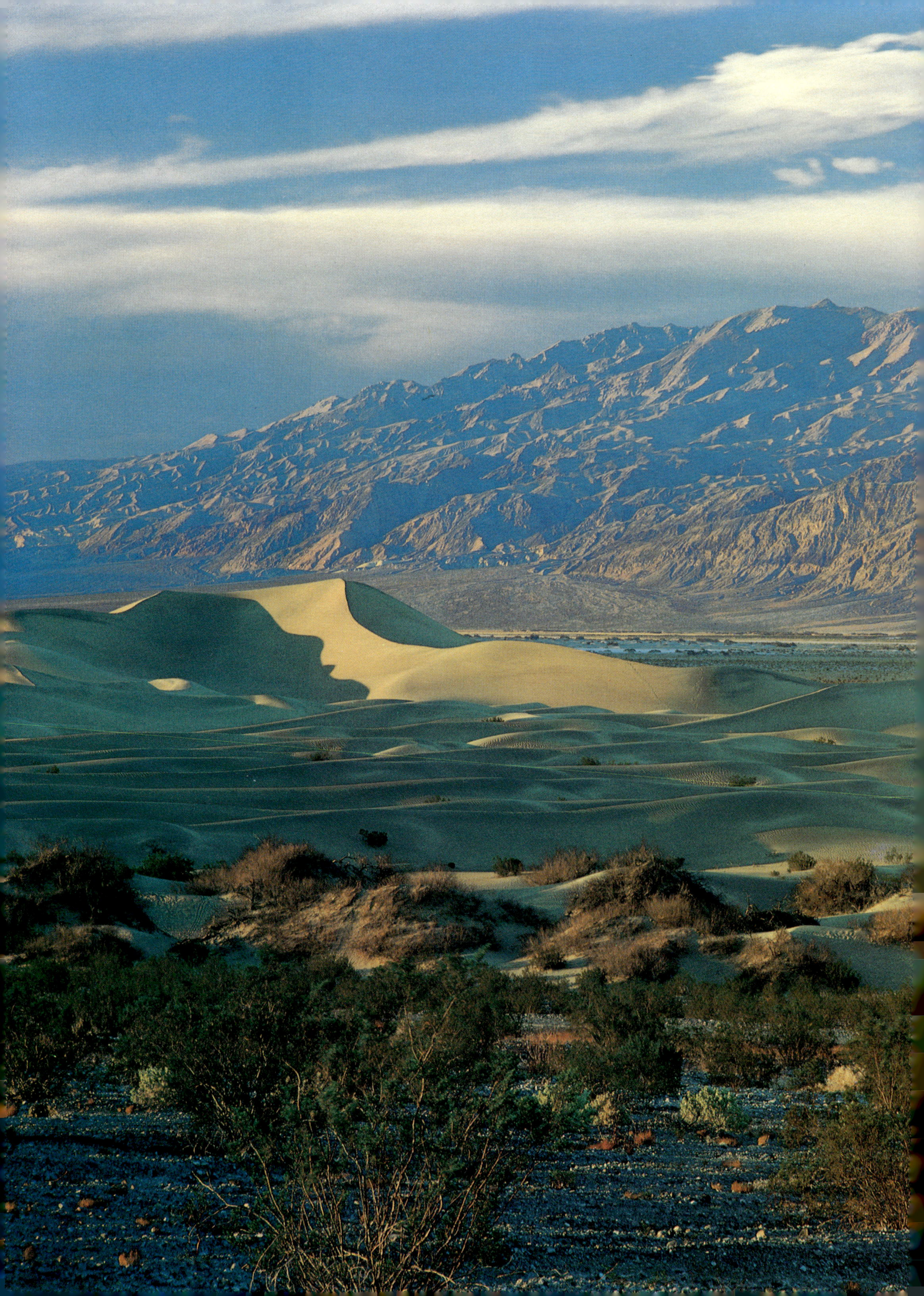

The Grapevine Mountains loom over the sand dunes in Death Valley National Monument.

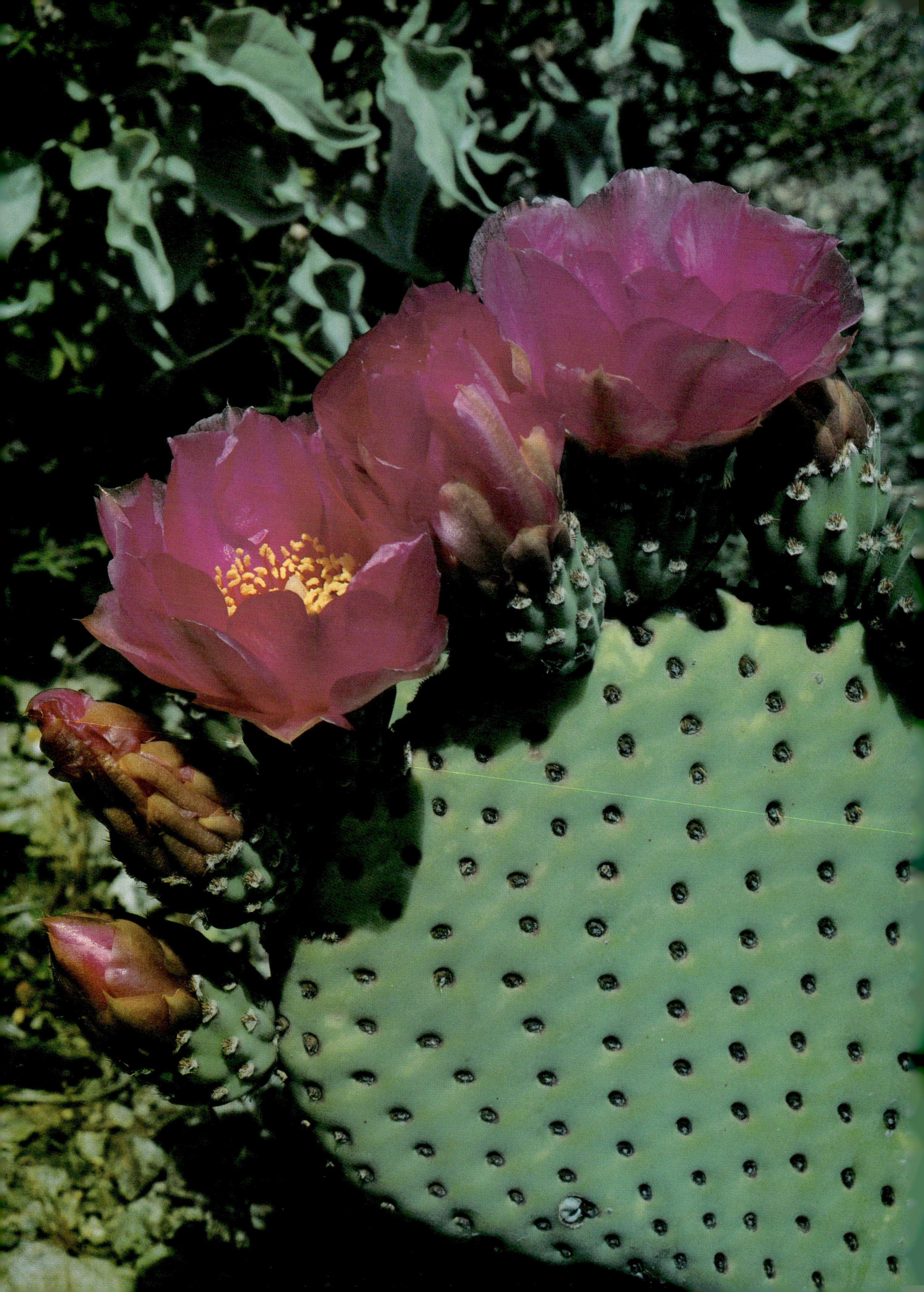

*Sand dunes near Cottonwood Mountains, Death Valley National Monument
(Following pages) Badwater, at 282 feet below sea level in Death Valley*

Beavertail cactus

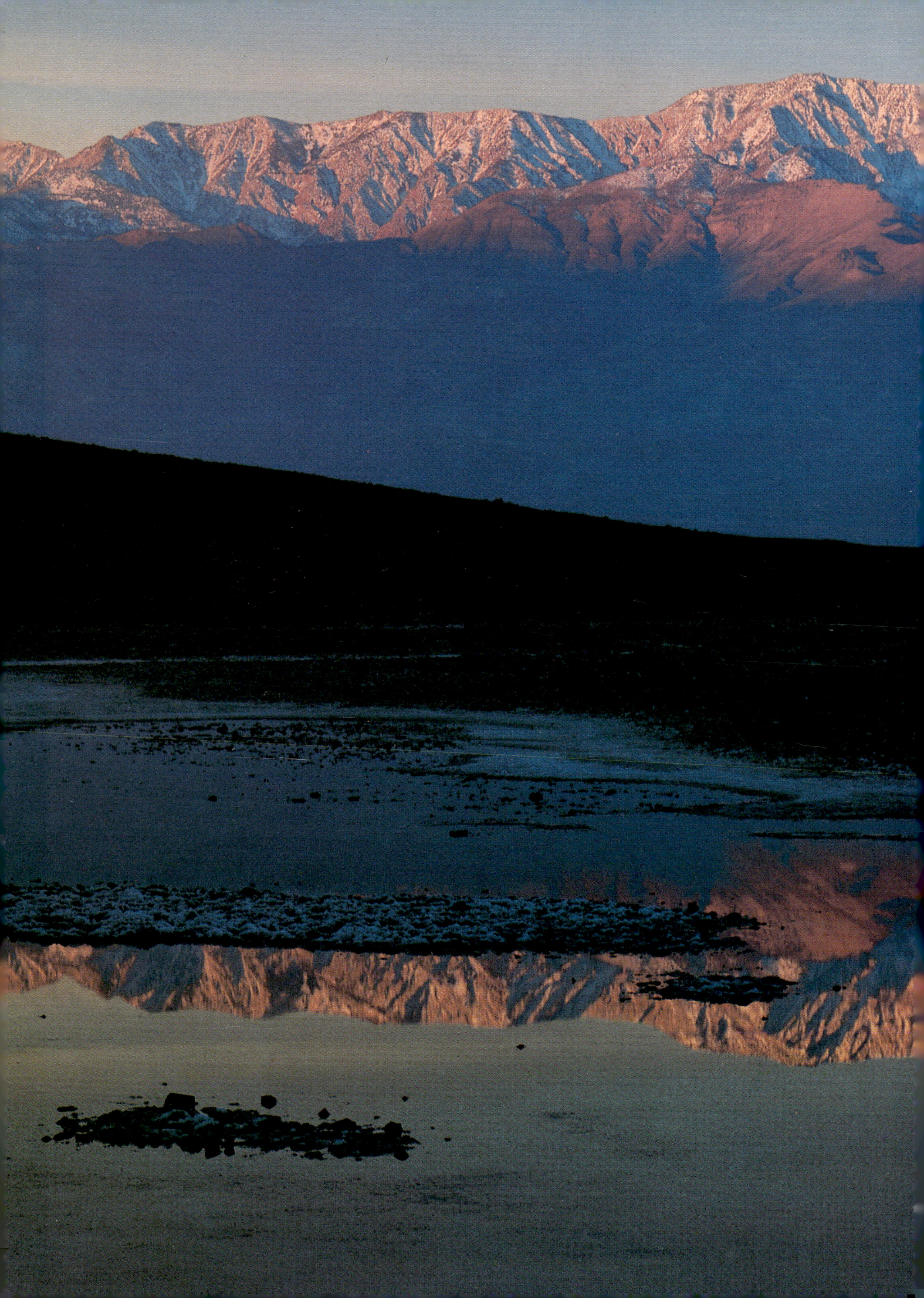

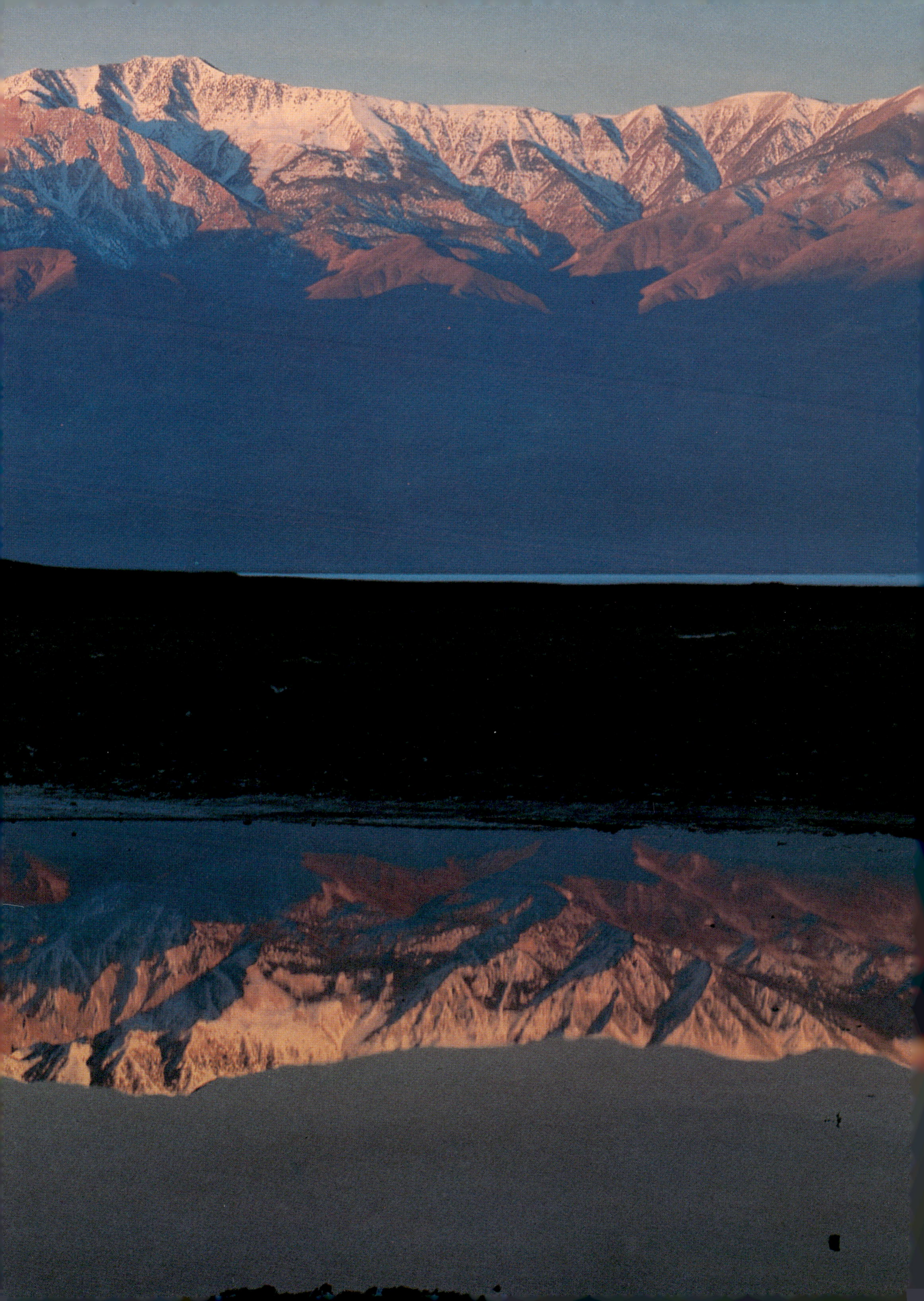

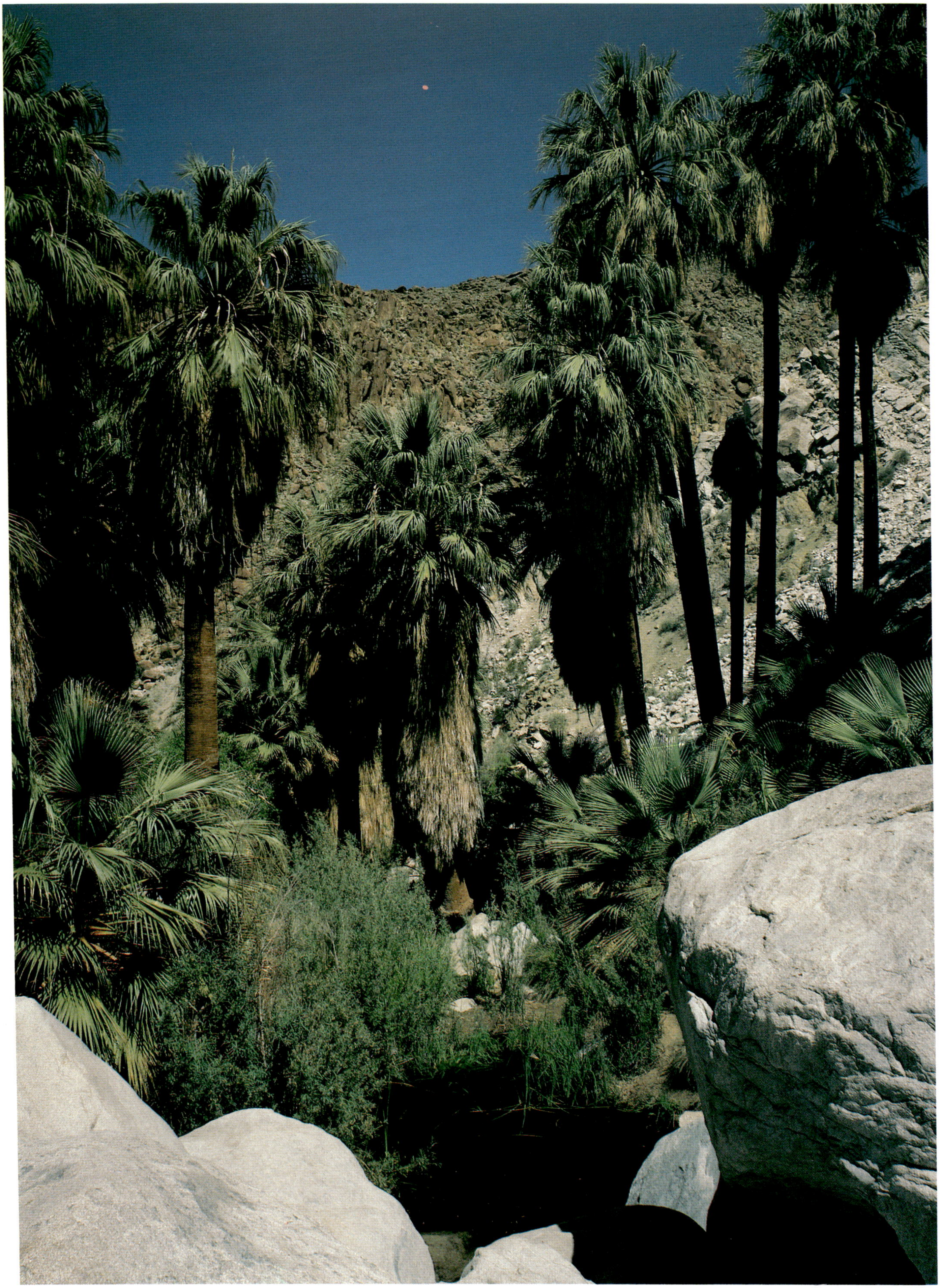

Mt. Whitney from the Alabama Hills

49 Palms Oasis, Joshua Tree National Monument

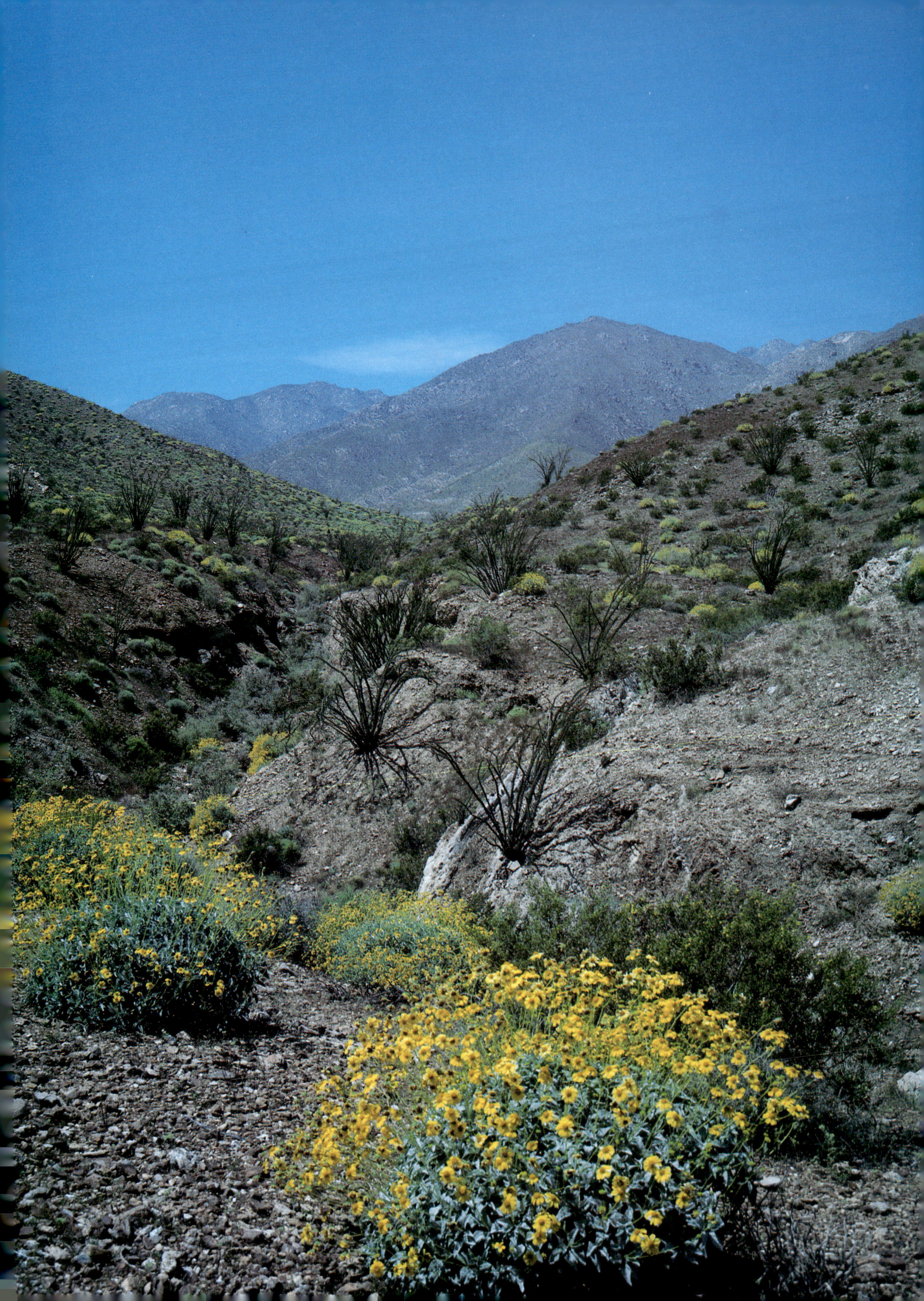

Mudstone Hills, 20 Mule Team Canyon, Death Valley National Monument

Anza-Borrego Desert

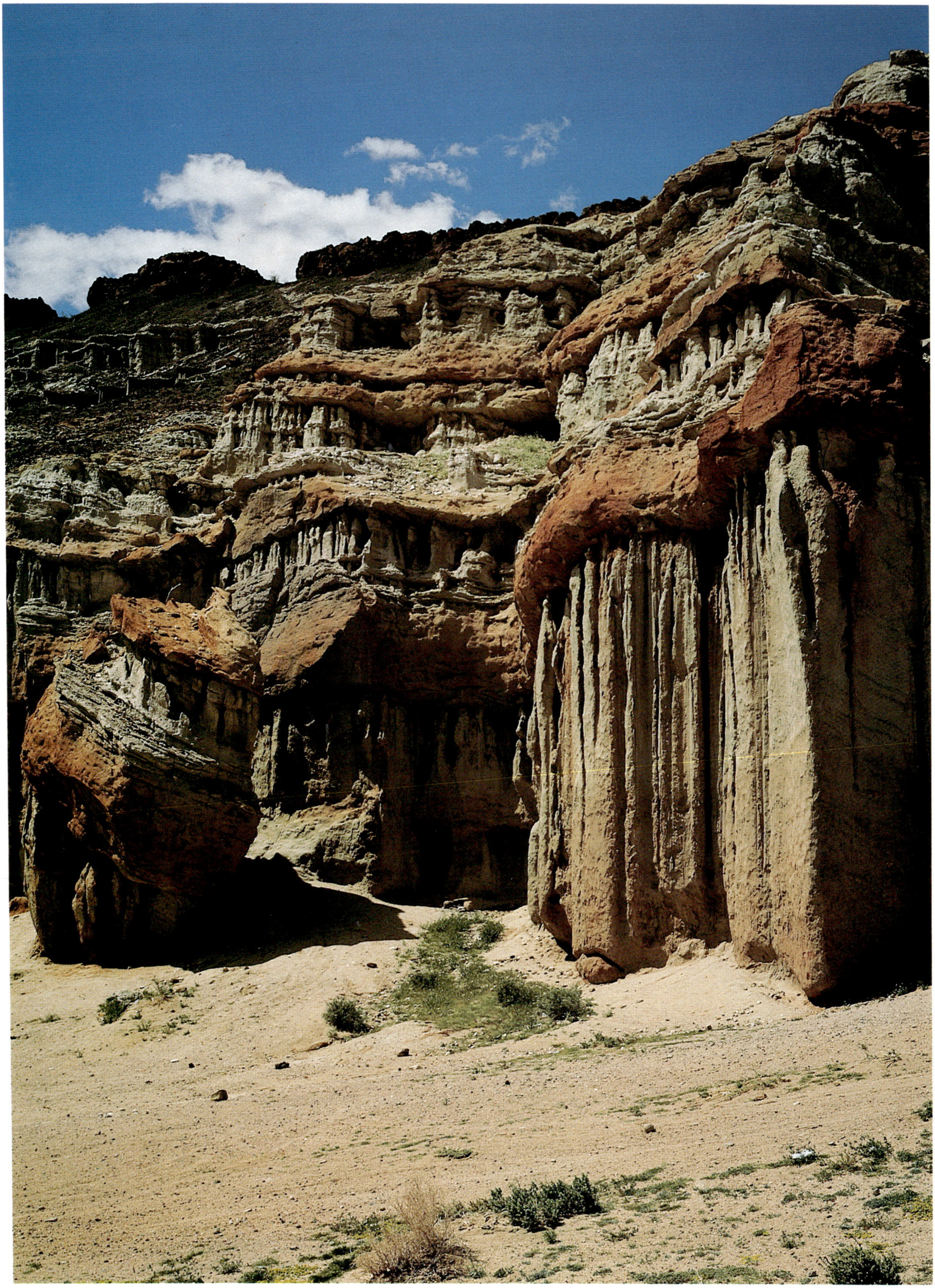

Joshua Tree National Monument

Red Rock Canyon, Mojave Desert

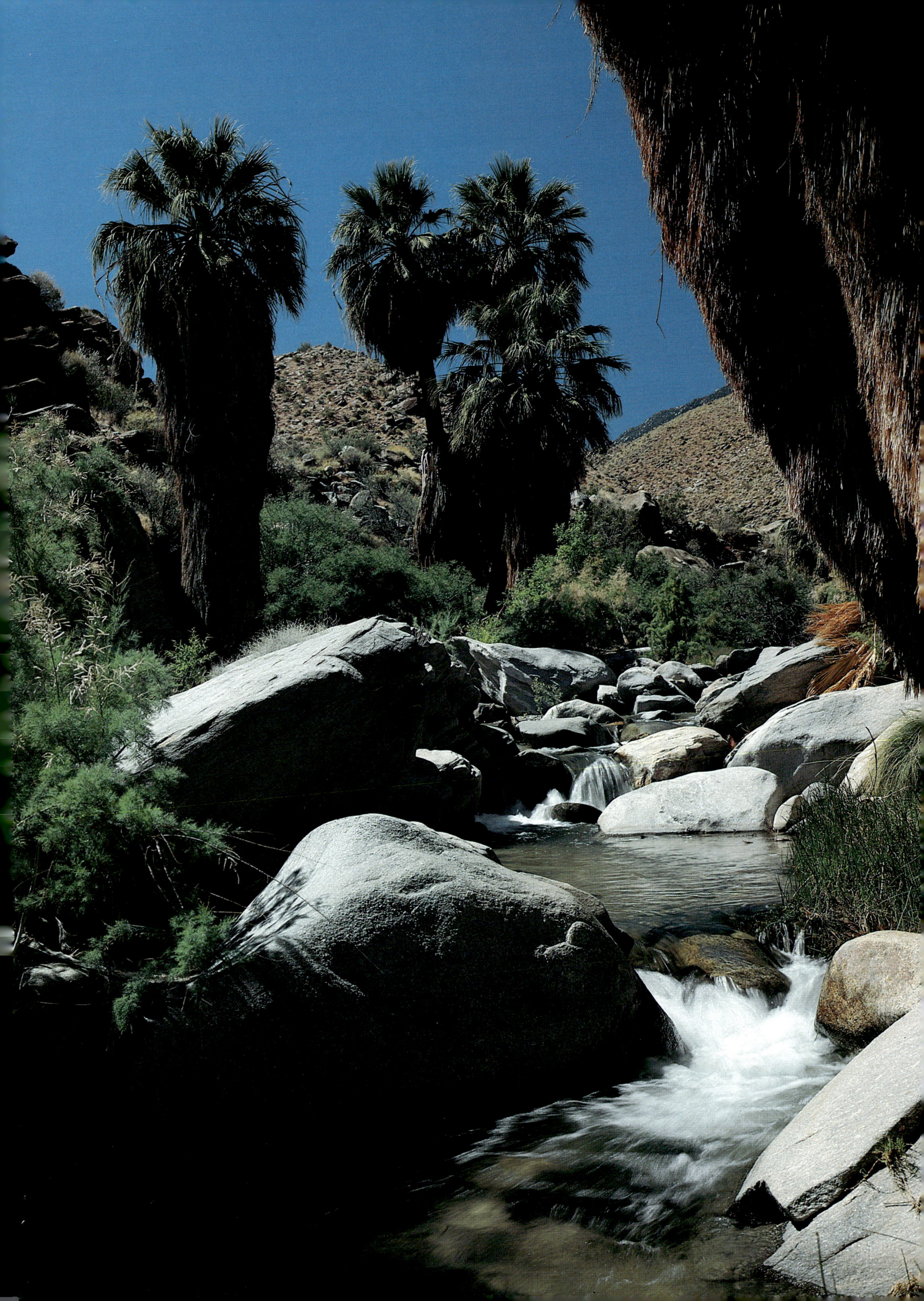

East Mojave Desert

Joshua Tree National Monument

Devil's Playground, East Mojave Desert
(Following pages) Mesquite Flat Dunes, Death Valley

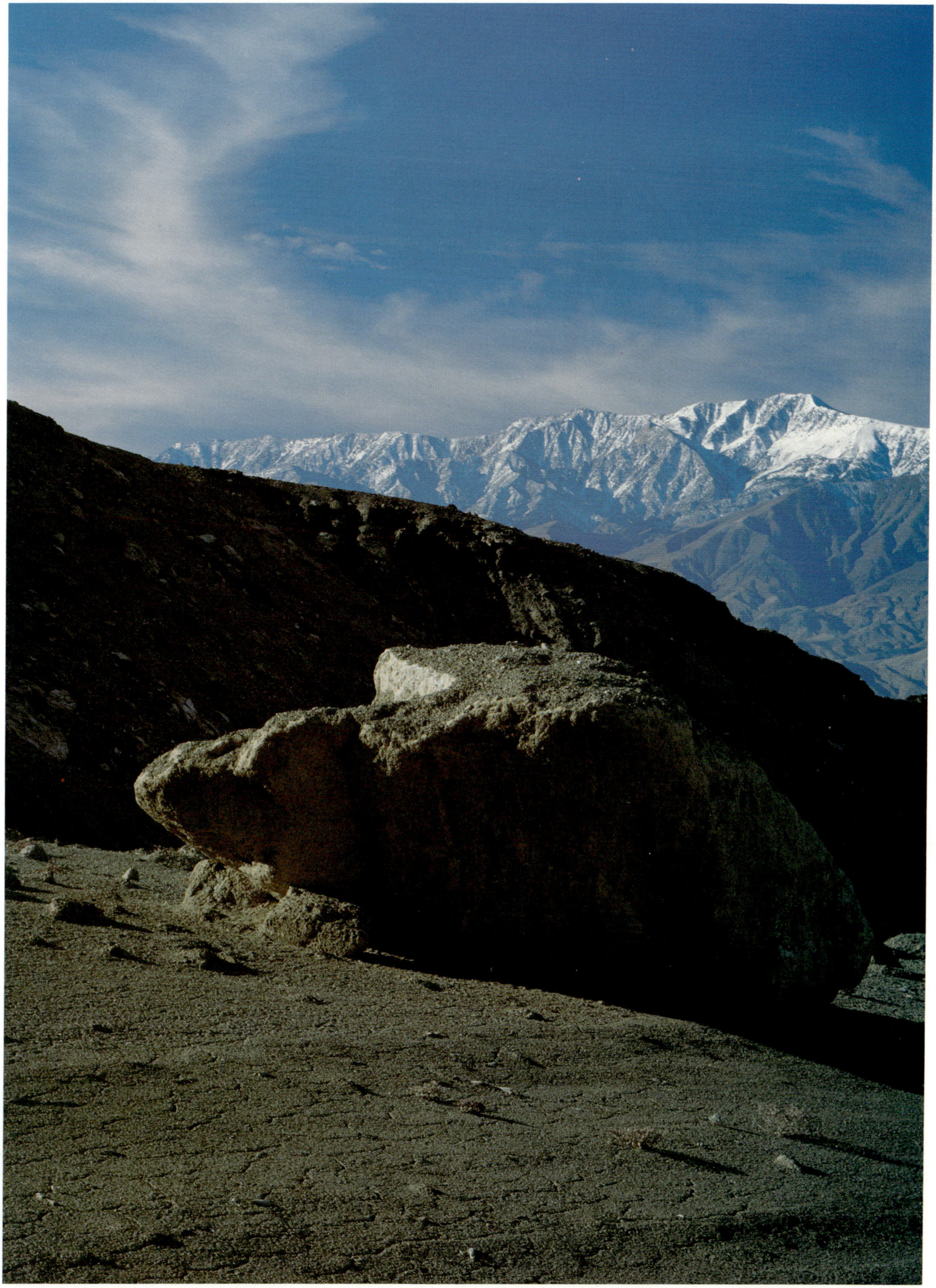

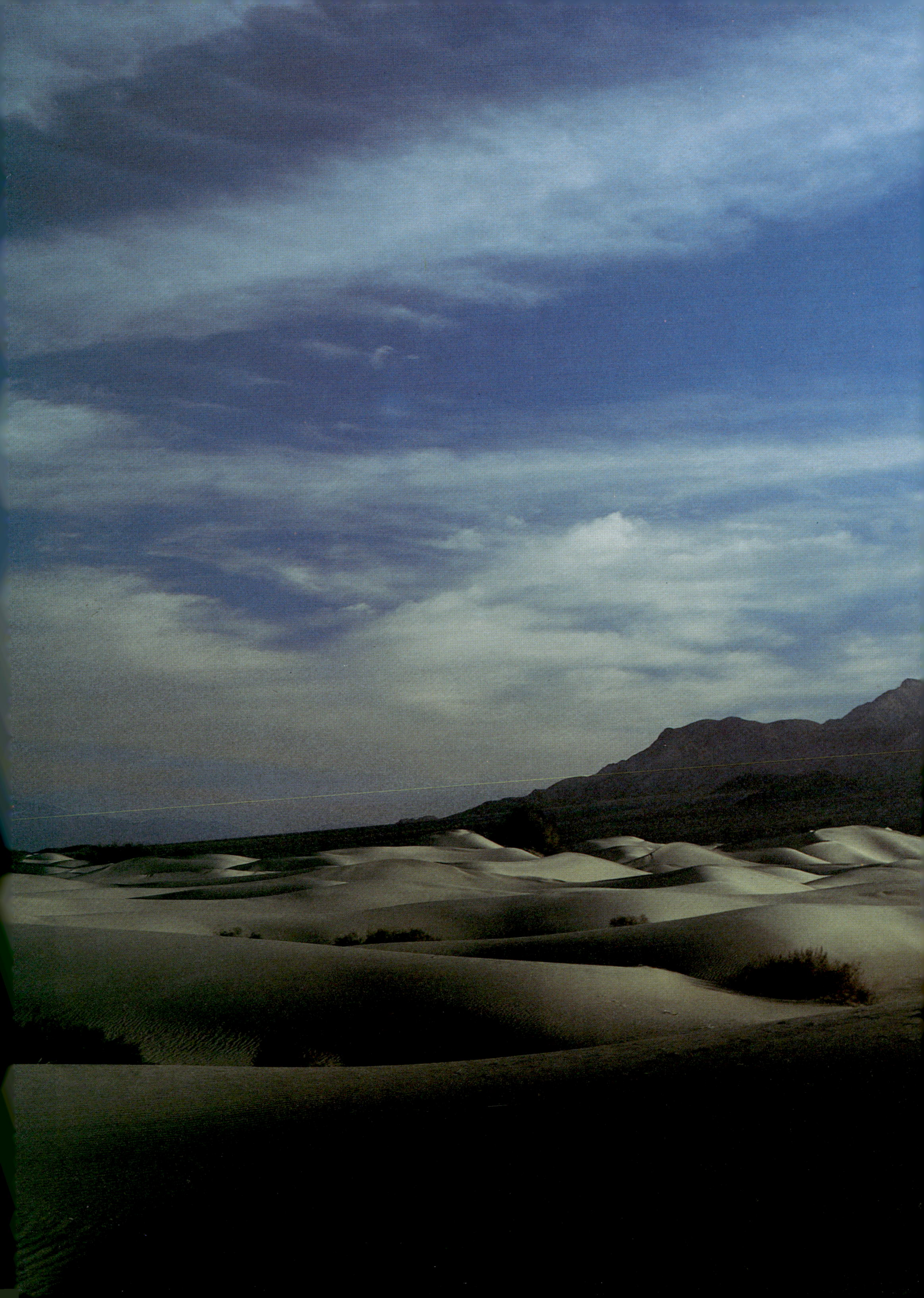

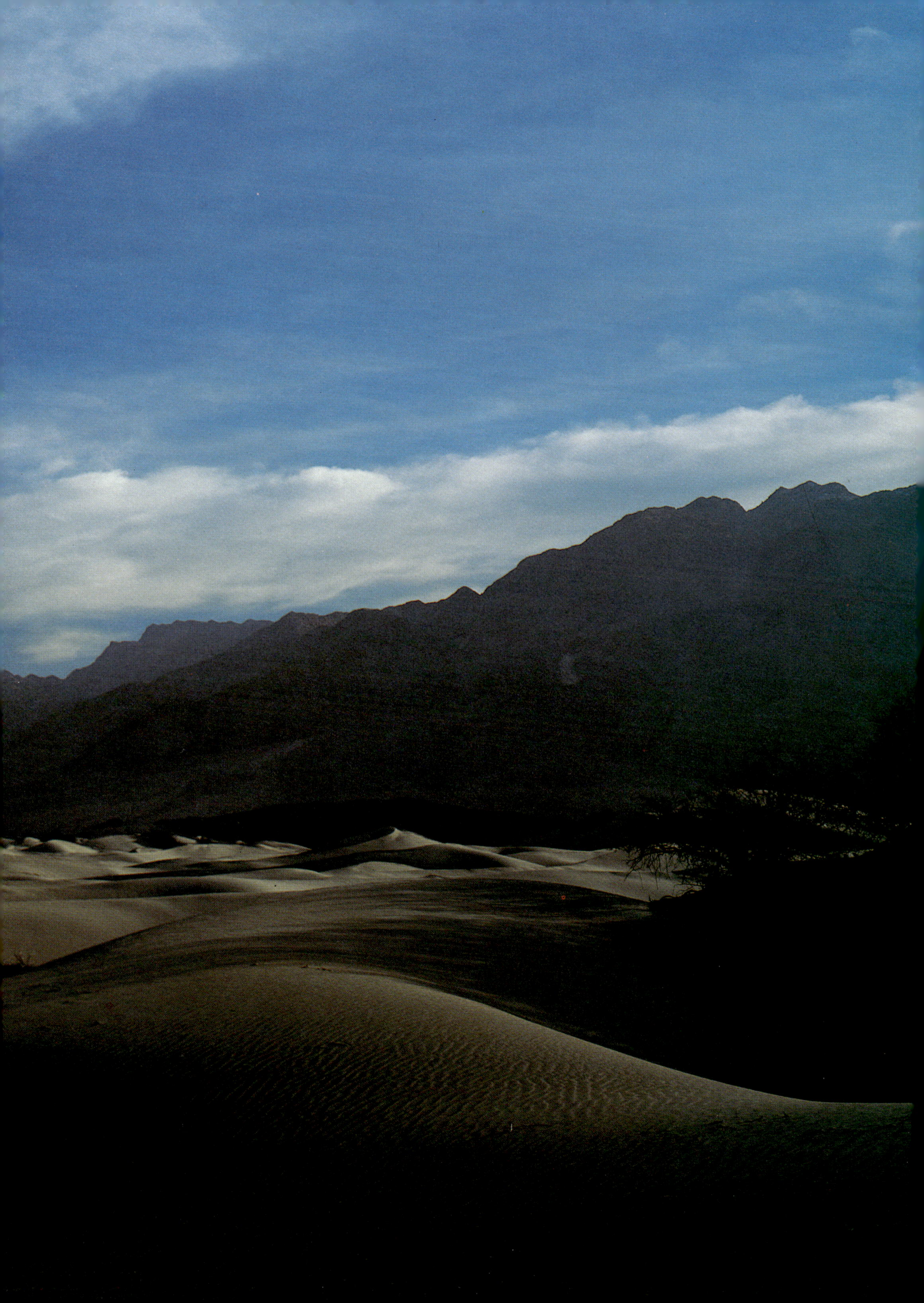

Mt. San Jacinto

Devil's Playground, East Mojave Desert
(Following pages) Cliffs of Emigrant Canyon, Death Valley National Monument

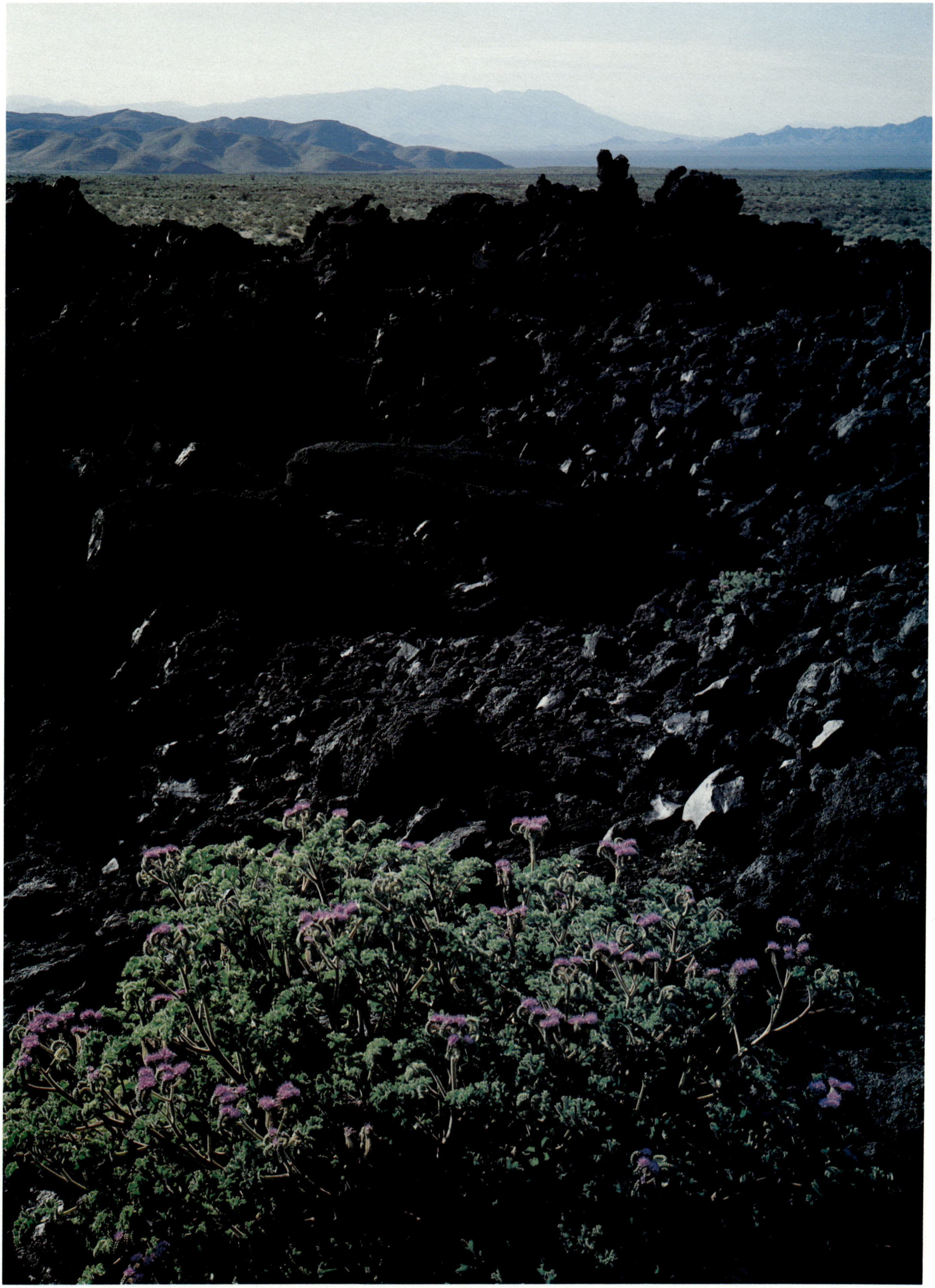

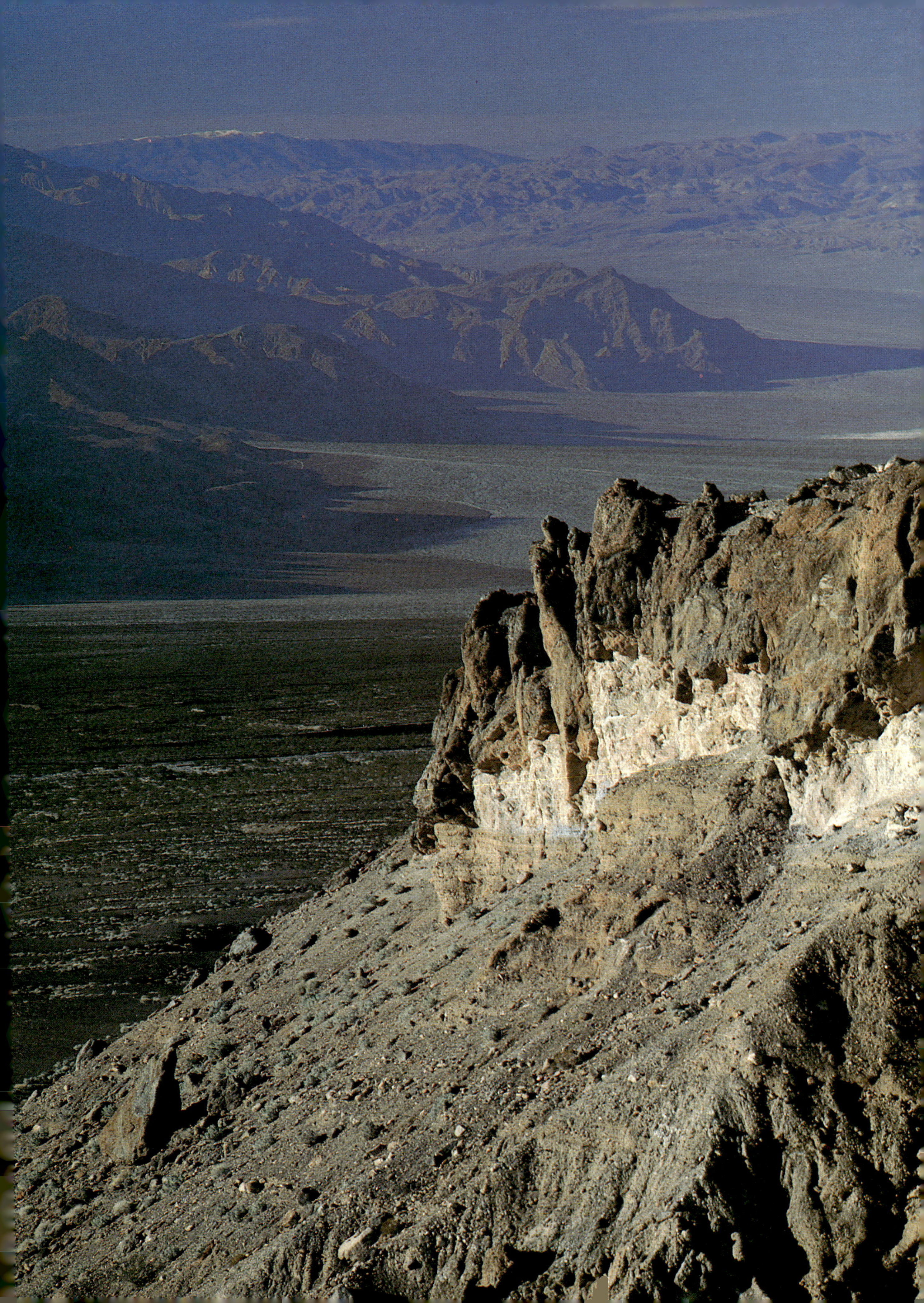

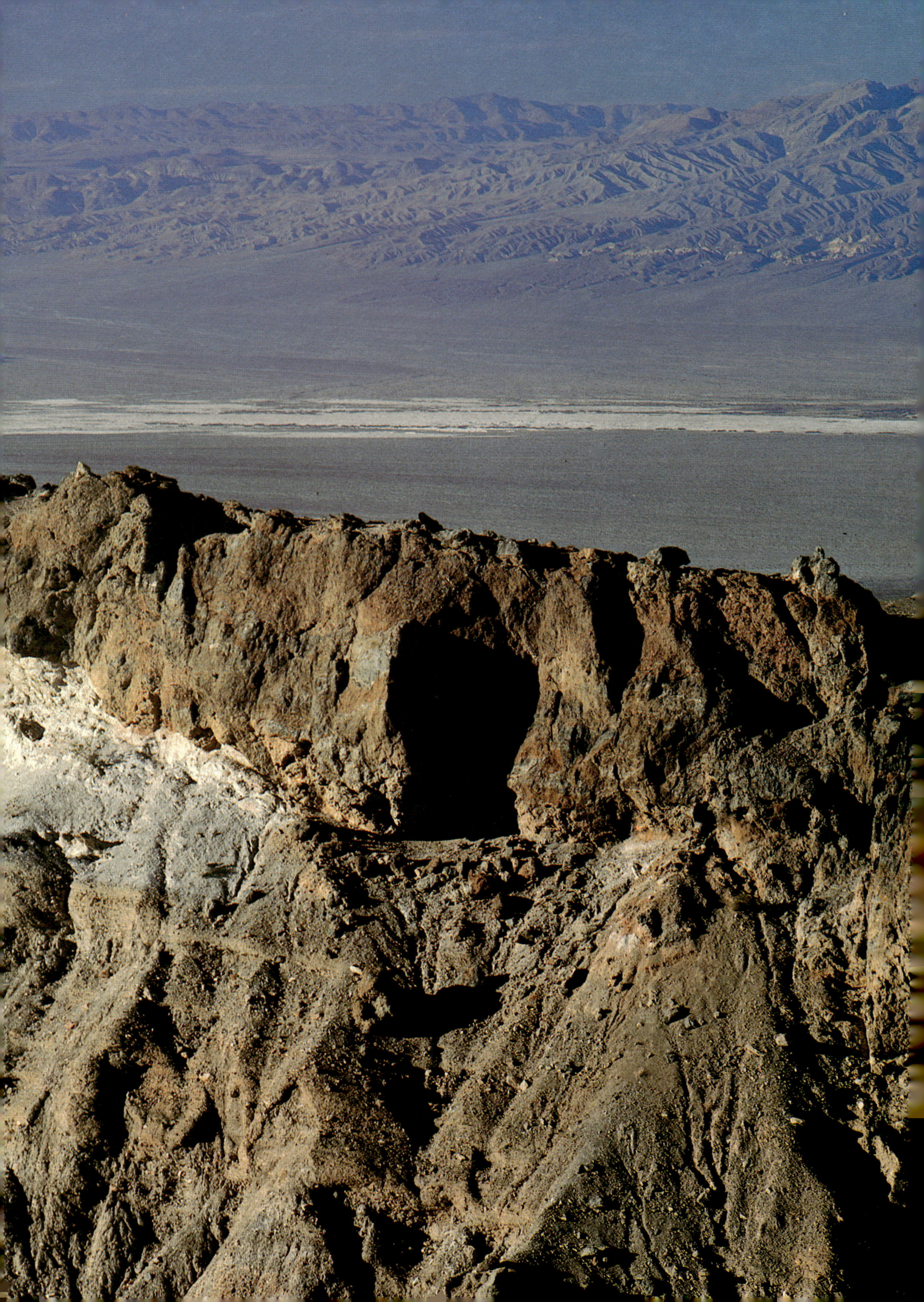

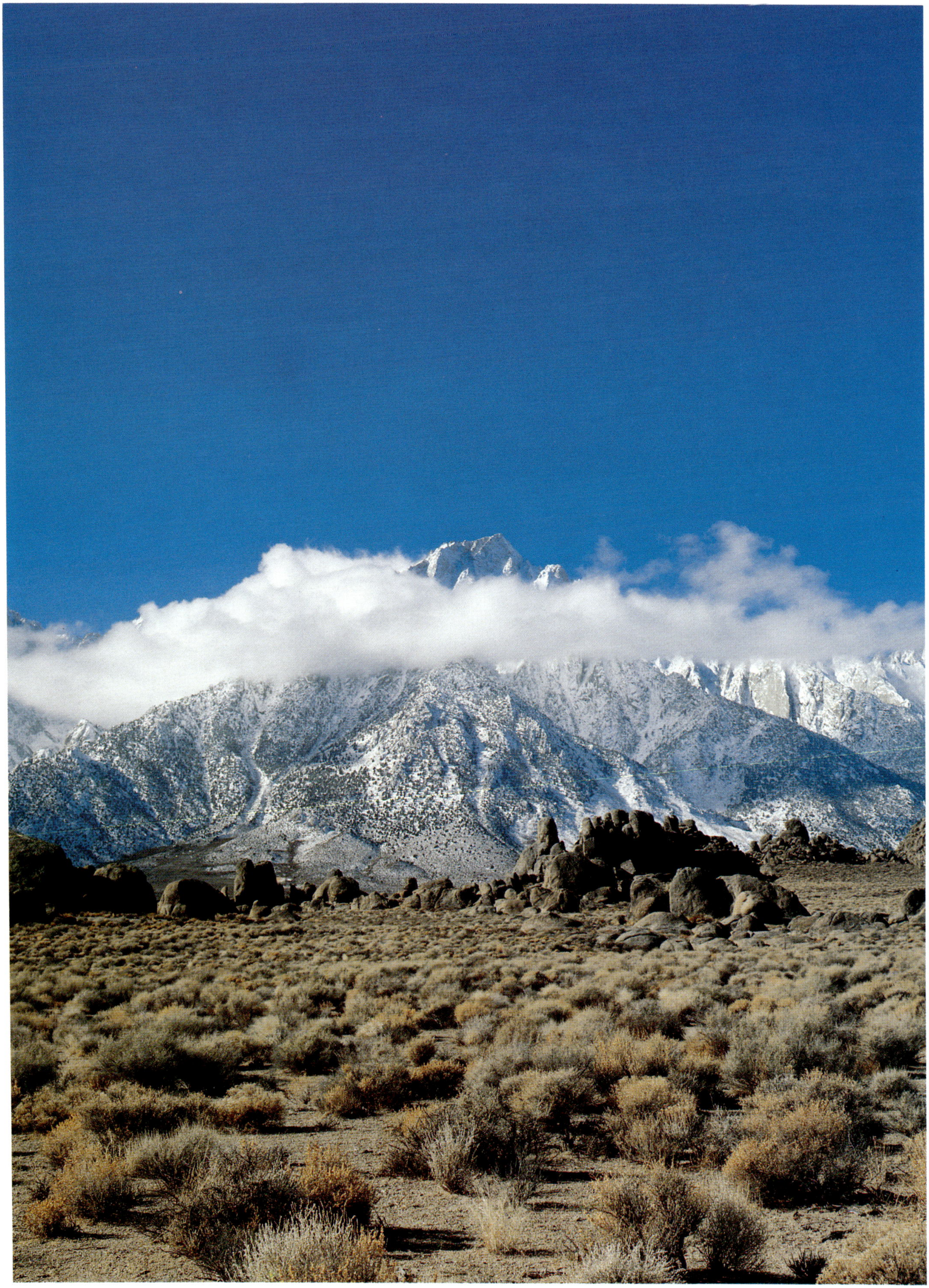

*Desert Primrose
(Following page) Waterfall in Palm Canyon
(Second following page) Stony Point*

Muir Crest from Alabama Hills in the Sierra Nevada Mountains

59

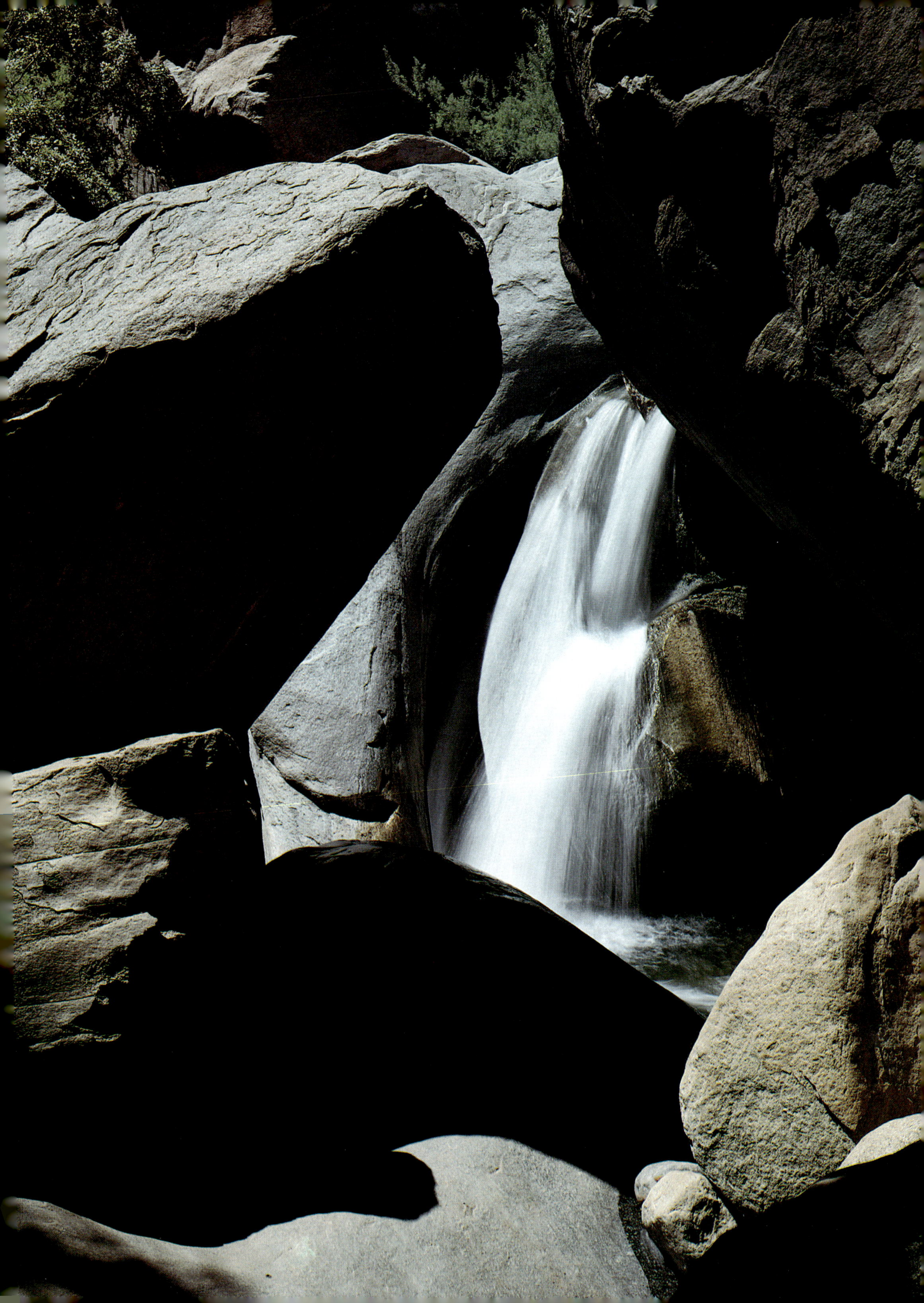

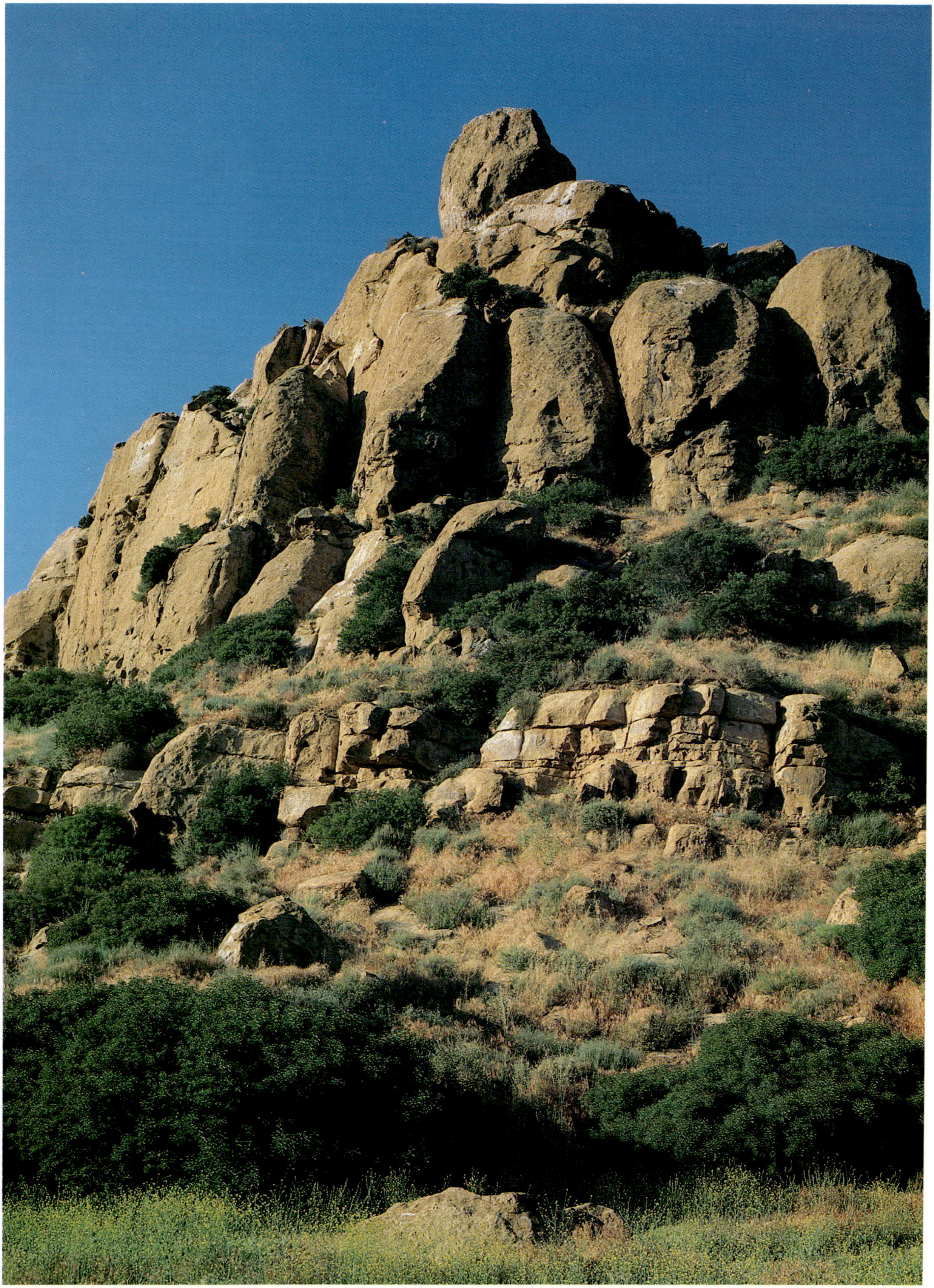

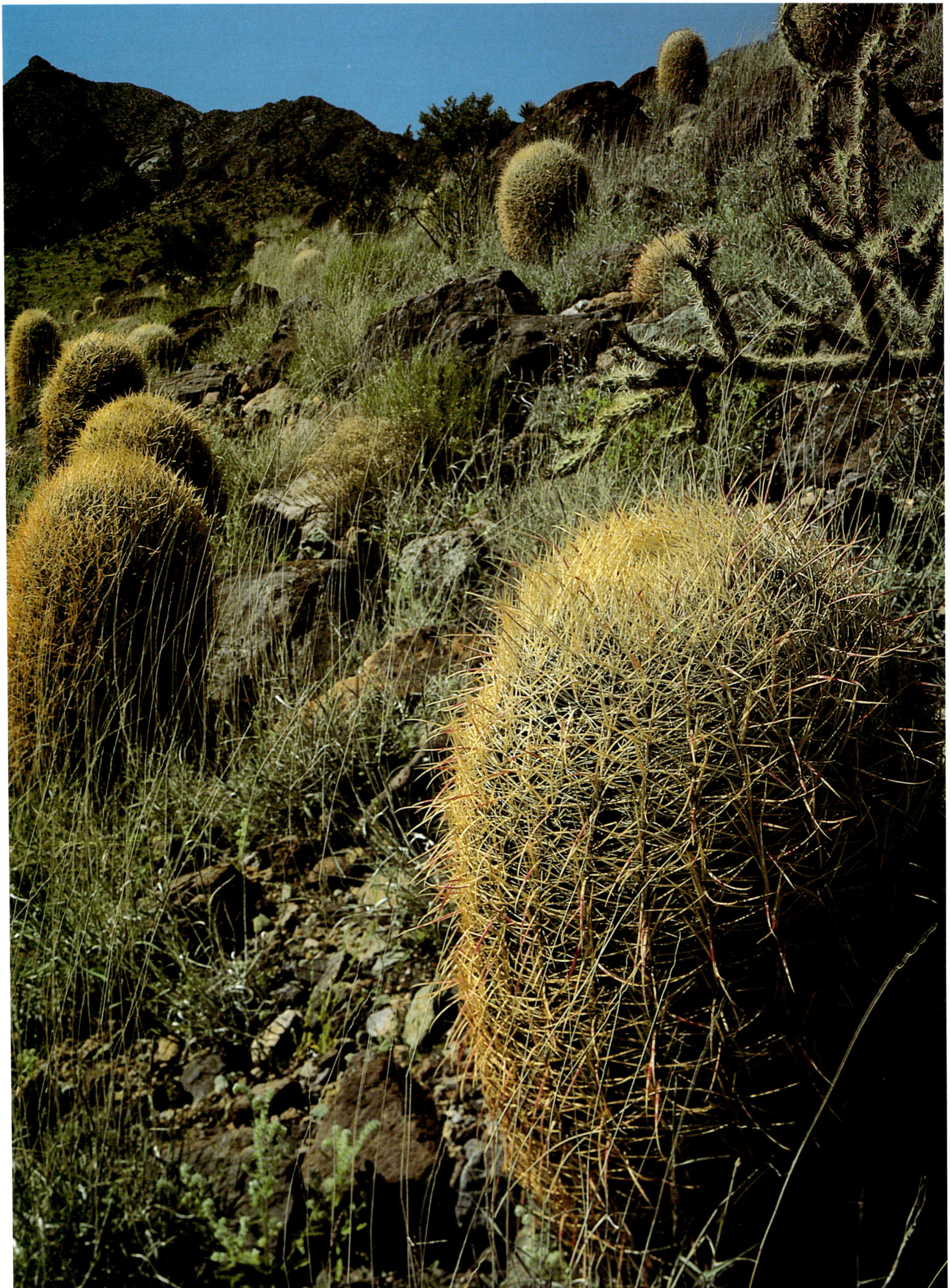

Sand dunes, Death Valley National Monument

Barrel cactus, Providence Mountains

Sunset, Joshua Tree National Monument

Joshua Tree National Monument

The Joshua tree, the naturalists tell us, is a lily of the family *Yucca brevifolia.* It is a desert plant, preferring the higher altitudes of the Mojave Desert. Its distinctive name most likely is an attribute of its distinctive appearance. The Biblical knowledge of the Mormon pioneers is apparently responsible for the name. The strange-appearing trees, with limbs turned up toward the heavens in an attitude of entreaty, invited an analogy with the Biblical Joshua.

Joshua Tree National Monument is located in a transitional zone between the high Mojave Desert and the low Colorado, so that it partakes of some aspects of both environments. The extensive forests of Joshua trees dominate the higher areas where they are found. But they are not all that is found in this very large preserve. The national monument harbors many kinds of flora and fauna within its 560,000 acres. While the Joshuas occupy open desert, Washingtonia palms are found in canyon washes. Pinon pine, creosote, yucca, and cactus are distributed widely according to altitudinal zones which favor the well-being of the particular plant species.

Desert creatures abound in Joshua Tree, even some you might not expect to find around a place where hard times would seem to be the accepted way of life. The kit foxes, coyotes, pack rats, squirrels, jackrabbits, and a variety of mouse species are more or less expected, but bighorn sheep, badgers, and bobcats also have found homes in the park. Many types of birds find this a good place to earn a livelihood; from golden eagles and turkey vultures, owls, roadrunners, and quail, to small birds like wrens and verdins.

The reptilian societies are well represented, too. The tortoise, the lizard, and the snake—including the desert rattlesnake varieties—are routinely seen in Joshua Tree. For a long time after the national monument was established in 1936 people left it pretty much alone. But in the sixties and seventies it began to receive heavy usage.

Easy access to this preserve is certainly one reason for its growing popularity. The monument stretches from a few miles northeast of Palm Springs far into the eastern Mojave Desert. It may be penetrated at several points from roads around its perimeter: Interstate 10 sweeps around its southern flank and state highways 62 and 177 on the west, north, and east complete the encircling road network. The park itself is quite primitive, but towns like Indio and Twentynine Palms on these roads are convenient launch points for potential park explorers. Taken together, the present population trends in Southern California and the ease of modern travel are making Joshua Tree National Monument one of the state's most popular recreational parks. Naturally it's more popular during the cooler seasons, when even the desert sometimes manages to get out of the hot sun. For solitude one has to do his visiting at night, which hinders visual appreciation, unless there's a full moon. On the other hand, a nighttime chorus of coyotes could bring to the visitor more of the desert's special poetry than is otherwise available.

But what does one "do" during a visit to a park where you have to pack in your own water and fuel, and where most areas are designated wilderness? There are "attractions" that draw the most visitors—places like Cottonwood Springs, or the Oasis of Mara at park headquarters. The Pinto Basin lies to the east, a low-desert region of the monument where Cholla cactus is abundant, having found the warmer climate to its liking. Another attraction is Salton View, one of the park's highest points at 5,185 feet, where the immense panorama of the desert spreads out far below, south to the Salton Sea and east to the stark unreality of San Gorgonio and San Jacinto peaks. But the best part is finding the lonely spots that still exist in the preserve, where you are the only visitor, and where you can take time to watch the life of the planet.

Death Valley National Monument

When we hear the name Death Valley, we rummage through our minds for a fact that we learned in school: Death Valley is the hottest place on earth. This is generally, if not literally, true. Death Valley's high so far has been recorded (in 1913) as 134.6°; a station in the Libyan desert has topped this by almost two degrees. Regardless of this, Death Valley, or some parts of it, manages to be hotter more often than any other part of the earth's surface. But the emphasis on heat is really unfair: we tend to dwell on the figure rather than on the time of year the reading was taken and on the obvious truth that seasonal and diurnal changes bring that hot reading down.

We remember, too, from our early geography books, that Death Valley has a very depressed salt flat near a place called Badwater which is the lowest point in the country—282 feet below sea level. We rarely remember that this young desert—younger than the Mojave—also has some very high points. Its extent of land below sea level is much less than the land mass of the Colorado Desert to the south that is in this category.

The monument was created in 1933, and its boundaries enclose 2,981 square miles. To have a valley you have to have mountains, and Death Valley's narrow trough winds 140 miles between high ranges with steep slopes, all included within the monument. The mountains that define the valley on the west are the Panamints. The Panamint Range has at times been called a "little Sierra." Its high points are from 6,000 to more than 11,000 feet, culminating in Telescope Peak, the highest mountain in Death Valley at 11,049 feet. The eastern wall is formed, north to south, by the Grapevine, Funeral, and Black Mountains. They top out at 8,000 feet.

Although Death Valley is sometimes identified, for convenience, with the Mojave Desert, geologists associate it with the Great Basin deserts that spread through parts of Oregon, Idaho, Utah, and Nevada. As recently as 25,000 years ago the long valley was occupied by a lake that was as much as 600 feet deep. The salty pond at Badwater is all that remains of this Ice Age phenomenon. But Death Valley is a kind of paradox. Its newness as a desert is in marked contrast to the age of some of its rocks. The precipitous west face of the Black Mountains at Dante's View reveals dark gneiss and schist that are considered among the oldest exposed rocks in the world. The age of these formations is put at one to two billion years.

One big reason for the existence of Death Valley stretches high and mighty west of the desert, with some intervening valleys. The Sierra Nevada looms over all. Its colossal eastern wall, awesome from any Death Valley view point, wrings out most of the moisture from Pacific storms, leaving the valley with one to two inches of rain annually. But even so, there is vegetation. In this severe test of life strategies, plants usually keep their distance from each other, so that each one has a better chance at what little moisture there is. There is no lack of nutrients. Deposits from ancient lakes and alluvium from the mountain ranges have filled the valley with thousands of feet of sediment. In addition to enduring lack of water, blowing desert wind, and scorching sun, desert plants have to be salt tolerant, too, because their growing medium is usually a salty *playa*, or basin. Desert lakes, having no drainage, have nowhere to go but up (by evaporation), so they leave behind all those alkaline minerals that accumulate during their existence.

Barren as it appears, then, Death Valley is a living community. The abundant creosote bush survives in the basins, as do saltbush and greasewood. The handsome desert holly can be seen spread across some alluvial slopes, specifically on Ubehebe Crater (at the valley's north end), where its little, silver-gray leaves are impressively displayed against the darker background of the cinder cone. Where conditions are cooler and the ground is higher, the Joshua tree appears here and there in isolated stands. The higher slopes also support pinon pine and juniper. At the pinnacle of the Death Valley life zones, on the heights of Telescope Peak, a few bristlecone pine trees stand like aged warriors from a mythical past.

Death Valley also is home to some of the rootless species. There are the crawlers: snakes and lizards; runners, such as coyotes, squirrels, jackrabbits, pack rats, kangaroo rats, and mice; fliers of many species: Gambel's quail roadrunners, owls, ravens, hawks, wrens, and so on. The migratory birds find Saratoga Springs at the valley's southern end to their liking. This desert oasis even has an ancient kind of aquatic life left over from the Ice Age: the inch-long pupfish, a species of killifish that lives in various wet spots scattered through the North American deserts. The pupfish, in

Death Valley and elsewhere, has demonstrated a near-magical ability to survive under incredible extremes of water temperature and salinity.

A legacy of man's early penetration of Death Valley are the wild burros—descendants of those once in the employ of the prospectors—that inhabit some of the mountain canyons. The prospectors and twenty-mule borax teams are gone (big-scale mining has taken over), and so are most of the other two-legged creatures. The rangers and park service personnel are the most numerous residents. The human population of this Sierra "backyard" lives mostly in the Owens Valley next to the big mountains.

The off-season for visits to Death Valley is obviously the hot one. It extends from June through October. One of the most pleasant months is December, although in winter the nights may reach the freezing point or below. The valley is now quite accessible. State 190 comes east from Owens Valley and goes through the heart of the monument. State 127 reaches north from I-15 at Baker, touching the monument's southern border and connecting with the other road at Death Valley Junction on the southeastern side. Secondary roads branch off from the primary valley highway to high view points and other places of scenic and historic interest.

The mountains that enclose Death Valley help to make it visually exciting not only by their massive presence and their rugged, rocky slopes but also by the range of color in their exposed flanks. These formations represent the total extent of geological life on earth. The Black Mountains are named for the cap of lava on their crown. But their black top is only the beginning of the color range in these mountains. A road to Dante's View does an end run around the northern flank of the Blacks, penetrating a canyon wash whose walls are rose, tawny, and pale green. Under the west slope of the range, another road takes an up-and-down route through another spectrum of up-tilted rocks, the variety of tints making inevitable the name, Artist's Palette.

The mountainscapes, the uptilted clay hills in the badlands area, the flowing, changing sand-dune sculptures, and the salt flats create continually fascinating and changing textures and colors as the sun moves across the heavens, selecting different aspects of the desert's landforms to highlight. Sunrise and sunset are especially prodigal of rich colorations and light-and-dark contrasts. When the high Panamint crest is dusted with snow during the winter, the orange-pink light of dawn touches the range with a special glory. Badwater, the salty pool below Dante's View, picks up all this and creates a second highlighted Panamint Range, upside-down. Telescope Peak lords it over the whole scene. Its summit is usually white with snow into May.

As the sun sets behind the Panamints, another startling change suffuses the valley. The ring of mountains becomes dusky silhouette, while the light of a still-bright sky picks out for a final goodbye scattered features of the desert's irregular floor. Badwater glows with a last silvery radiance before it, too, disappears with the vanishing day.

Dante's View probably offers the widest panorama of Death Valley from a place that's handy to get to. Both the lowest and highest points in the country (the coterminous states) are within the compass of this vantage point: the valley floor near Badwater (-282 feet) and over on the skyline, Mt. Whitney (14,495 feet). At Zabriskie Point, farther north on the mountains, is another stretched-out view of the desert's many shapes and colors. On the salt beds below Zabriskie, a nearby area has been dubbed the Devil's Golf Course, because of its fiendish appearance. The salt basin is riddled with grotesque pillars and ridges that crystallized out of the waters of the ancient lake and are still being formed through evaporation of upward-welling ground water.

Another sinister name is applied to a desert spot some 25 miles farther north in the valley. The Devil's Cornfield is the fanciful label for a field of desert shrubbery pushed and teased by wind and sand into growing like corn shocks. The famous Mesquite Flat Sand Dunes occupy 25 square miles of the northern valley, and are defined in a soft, undulating pattern of sinuous curves that ascend and descend in a tableau of arrested motion. Near the dunes, Stovepipe Wells village accommodates thirsty desert travelers in the tradition of the original desert water holes in this spot. During early crossing of the desert the water found here was a life-saver on many occasions. To prevent the holes from disappearing under the blowing sand, the spot was marked by a stove pipe.

The Panamint Range on the west, being the highest mountains in the neighborhood, have their own quota of good view points. One of these is Auguerreberry Point, about 6,000 feet up. The picture of Death Valley from this side is best in the afternoon, just as the outlook from the east side's Black Mountains, is best in the morning. Auguerreberry Point looks out not only over the multicolored desert but to the far horizon into Nevada; due east, 80 miles away, Charleston Peak can be seen. For the very pinnacle of scenic opportunities in Death Valley, there is the top of Telescope Peak itself. One may get within six miles of the summit at Mahogany Flat, where the automobile road ends. From there on it's hoofing it up the trail.

The Grapevine Mountains close in the northeast corner of Death Valley. A road that parallels the Grapevines provides access to the monument's northern extremity. Here are two noteworthy creations, one natural and one man-made. The cinder pile Ubehebe Crater, in the former category, is an 800-foot-deep, half-mile-wide cone that spread a lot of fire and brimstone around the valley not far back in geological time. The latter phenomenon, the man-made one, is Scotty's Castle, the elaborate Spanish provincial dwelling built by the eccentric Death Valley Scotty (Walter Scott) in this unlikely location. It is reached by a side road through Grapevine Canyon, about three miles.

A desert like Death Valley, spectacular by day, becomes an enchanted land at night. The summer heat softens to warmth; other times it can be downright chilly. The nighttime stillness seems accentuated by the somber shadows of near and far mountains. If there is a moon, the dunes and other prominences on the desert floor turn phosphorescent in its pale light. Most desert creatures are on the night shift. They hide away from the sun's furnace heat during the day and venture out usually when darkness comes to earn their living. Their scuttlings and scurryings may be heard by a careful listener. Observation by sight is not very likely unless there is bright moonlight. Whether the visitor camps out in Death Valley and experiences its magic in this way, or whether he explores it from the more formal precincts of a desert lodging, the quiet and fragrance of the desert under a star-filled sky will bring refreshment for his senses and balm for his soul.

Beautiful America Publishing Company

The nation's foremost publisher of quality color photography

Current Books

Alaska	Maryland	Oregon Vol. II
Arizona	Massachusetts	Oregon Coast
Boston	Michigan	Oregon Country
British Columbia	Michigan Vol. II	Pacific Coast
California	Minnesota	Pennsylvania
California Vol. II	Missouri	Pittsburgh
California Coast	Montana	San Diego
California Desert	Montana Vol. II	San Francisco
California Missions	Monterey Peninsula	San Juan Islands
California Mountains	Mormon	Seattle
Chicago	Mt. Hood (Oregon)	Tennessee
Colorado	Nevada	Texas
Dallas	New Jersey	Utah
Delaware	New Mexico	Utah Country
Denver	New York	Vancouver U.S.A.
Florida	New York City	Vermont
Georgia	Northern California	Virginia
Hawaii	Northern California Vol. II	Volcano Mt. St. Helens
Idaho	North Carolina	Washington
Illinois	North Idaho	Washington Vol. II
Indiana	Ohio	Washington, D.C.
Kentucky	Oklahoma	Wisconsin
Las Vegas	Orange County	Wyoming
Los Angeles, 200 Years	Oregon	Yosemite National Park

Forthcoming Books

Alabama	Kauai	Oahu
Arkansas	Maine	Phoenix
Baltimore	Maui	Rhode Island
Connecticut	Mississippi	Rocky Mountains
Detroit	New England	South Carolina
The Great Lakes	New Hampshire	South Dakota
Houston	North Dakota	West Virginia
Kansas		

Large Format, Hardbound Books

Beautiful America	Beauty of Washington	Lewis & Clark Country
Beauty of California	Glory of Nature's Form	Western Impressions
Beauty of Oregon	Volcanoes of the West	

For a complete product catalog, send $1.00.
Beautiful America Publishing Company
P.O. Box 608
Beaverton, Oregon 97075